QUIZSHEETS

A selection of 80 themed, photocopyable quiz sheets.

By Graham Redman

These sheets should be useful to anybody who writes pub quizzes or a quiz for a charity fund-raising event, or they can be used as a bank of questions, or even just to challenge yourself. They are designed to be photocopied as a written quiz and hence they have spaces for the answers and team names. There are 80 sheets with an average of about 25 questions on each, that's over 2000 questions. They are called 'Half Time Quiz' because you can use them for the written part of the quiz which is usually handed in at 'half time' or the interval for marking. This is the part of the quiz that can take much longer to compile.

authorHOUSE®

AuthorHouse™ UK Ltd.
1663 Liberty Drive
Bloomington, IN 47403 USA
www.authorhouse.co.uk
Phone: 0800.197.4150

Published by AuthorHouse 11/11/2013

ISBN: 978-1-4918-8135-4 (sc)
ISBN: 978-1-4918-8136-1 (e)

This book is printed on acid-free paper.

A note about the author

I am a retired teacher from Kent having spent nearly forty years teaching children of all ages from nine upwards, mainly maths, science and IT.

I am a member of a quiz team and we attend two pub quizzes on a regular basis. About three years ago at one of them, the ladies running it asked if anyone would like to contribute a half time quiz sheet as they were very pressed for time that week. I took up the challenge and have been doing it ever since, so now I have a large collection of available sheets. Usually I choose a theme and design the quiz sheet round it.

When I am not writing quiz sheets I spend my time walking, growing my own vegetables and visiting heritage sites with my camera. I also work for a charity called 'Beanstalk' helping children to learn to read.

This book is dedicated to my wife, Janet, and the other members of my quiz team, Gill, Rosemary and Di. Also to Jan and Linda who raise thousands of pounds each year for a cancer charity through their weekly quiz.

List of Quiz Sheets

1. HALF TIME QUIZ   TEAM NAME _____

Since 1934 there has always been an OSCAR awarded for the best song featured in a film for each year. Some of these songs have sunk into obscurity but many have become well known and some of them classics. Below are 25 films together with their Oscar winning year, all you have to do is identify the song than won.

	YEAR	FILM	OSCAR WINNING SONG
Ex.	1934	The Gay Divorcee	*The Continental*
1.	1936	Swing Time	
2.	1939	The Wizard of Oz	
3.	1940	Pinocchio	
4.	1942	Holiday Inn	
5.	1944	Going My Way	
6.	1947	The Song of the South	
7.	1952	High Noon	
8.	1953	Calamity Jane	
9.	1956	The Man Who Knew Too Much	
10.	1961	Breakfast at Tiffany's	
11.	1964	Mary Poppins	
12.	1967	Doctor Doolittle	
13.	1968	The Thomas Crown Affair	
14.	1969	Butch Cassidy & the Sundance Kid	
15.	1982	An Officer & a Gentleman	
16.	1983	Flashdance	
17.	1984	The Woman in Red	
18.	1986	Top Gun	
19.	1987	Dirty Dancing	
20.	1989	The Little Mermaid	
21.	1992	Aladdin	
22.	1993	Philadelphia	
23.	1994	The Lion King	
24.	1997	Titanic	
25.	2008	Slumdog Millionaire	

2. HALF TIME QUIZ   TEAM NAME_____

'Show biz' people frequently have stage names because they sound better. What are the stage names of the 25 people whose real names are listed. They are a mixture of British and American actors and musicians and other celebrities, some going back quite a few years. They are in no particular order.

	REAL NAME	STAGE NAME
Ex.	David White	*David Jason*
1.	Bernard Schwartz	
2.	Marshall Bruce Mathers	
3.	Marion Morrison	
4.	Daniel Kaminski	
5.	Antoine Domino	
6.	Barbara Ann Deeks	
7.	Robert Zimmerman	
8.	Charles Hardin Holley	
9.	Richard Starkey	
10.	Frances Gumm	
11.	Susan Weaver	
12.	Maurice Micklewhite	
13.	Richard Grant Esterhuysen	
14.	Norman Cook	
15.	Pricilla White	
16.	Marie McDonald	
17.	Doris Kappelhoff	
18.	Reginald Dwight	
19.	Neville Holder	
20.	Gordon Sumner	
21.	Arnold Dorsey	
22.	Archibald Leech	
23.	Norma Jeane Baker	
24.	Shirley Crabtree	
25.	Lionel Begleiter	

In the celebrity list below there are ten names. Five are stage names and the rest are their real names. Can you pick out the celebrities with five REAL names and list them at the bottom.

Julie Andrews
David Bowie
Matt Damon
Johnny Depp
Neil Diamond
Clint Eastwood
Anthony Hopkins
Ben Kingsley
Elaine Paige
Catherine Tate

1. _____

2. _____

3. _____

4. _____

5. _____

3. HALF TIME QUIZ TEAM NAME_____

'Sit-coms' are very popular on both ITV and BBC. All you have to do is identify the principal star or stars in each of the following comedy programs. Remember it is the cast leaders we are looking for, not just anyone who may have appeared in the program. The number in the second box indicates how many names you need to write down.   <u>EXAMPLE</u>

	Only Fools and Horses	2	*David Jason & Nicholas Lyndhurst*

1.	My Family	2	
2.	One Foot in the Grave	2	
3.	Home to Roost	1	
4.	To the Manor Born	2	
5.	For the Love of Ada	2	
6.	Rising Damp	1	
7.	Keeping up Appearances	1	
8.	In Loving Memory	1	
9.	The Likely Lads	2	
10.	Oh No it's Selwyn Froggitt	1	
11.	As Time Goes By	2	
12.	Fawlty Towers	2	
13.	Never the Twain	2	
14.	Butterflies	2	
15,	Goodnight Sweetheart	1	
16.	Open All Hours	2	
17.	Waiting for God	2	
18.	Yes Minister	2	
19.	Ever Decreasing Circles	1	
20.	Steptoe and Son	2	
21.	George and Mildred	2	
22.	Nearest and Dearest	2	
23.	After You've Gone	2	
24.	May to September	1	

4. HALF TIME QUIZ   TEAM NAME_____

You need to find the names of child actors who performed in the films listed. All of them were under the age of 18 when they appeared in the film named. Some went on to become well known adult performers. As well as the film you will be given their initials, gender and the age they were when they made the film.

	INITIALS	FILM	GENDER	AGE	ANSWER
1.	JA	The Railway Children 1970	F	17	
2.	DB	ET 1982	F	7	
3.	FB	Little Lord Fauntleroy 1936	M	12	
4.	JB	Billy Elliot 2000	M	14	
5.	JC	The Kid 1921	M	7	
6.	MC	Home Alone 1990	M	10	
7.	KD	Mary Poppins 1964	F	9	
8.	JF	Bugsy Malone 1976	F	14	
9.	JG	Love Finds Andy Hardy 1938	F	16	
10.	RG	Harry Potter & the Chamber of Secrets 2002	M	14	
11.	SJ	Home Alone 3 1997	F	13	
12.	KK	Bend it Like Beckham 2002	F	17	
13.	BL	Bugsy Malone 1976	F	12	
14.	RM	The King's Speech 2010	F	9	
15.	ML	Oliver 1968	M	10	
16.	LL	The Parent Trap 1998	F	12	
17.	HM	Pollyanna 1960	F	8	
18.	AN	Oliver Twist 1948	M	17	
19.	TO'N	Paper Moon 1973	F	10	
20.	RP	The Mosquito Coast 1986	M	16	
21.	DR	Harry Potter & the Chamber of Secrets 2002	M	13	
22.	MR	Little Lord Fauntleroy 1936	M	16	
23.	WR	Beetlejuice 1988	F	17	
24.	ET	National Velvet 1944	F	12	
25.	ST	Baby Take a Bow 1934	F	6	
26.	EW	Harry Potter & the Chamber of Secrets 2002	F	12	
27.	JW	Oliver 1968	M	15	
28.	MW	Mrs Doubtfire 1993	F	6	
29.	NW	Rebel Without a Cause 1955	F	17	

5. HALF TIME QUIZ   TEAM NAME _____

You have to find the name of the films that were- awarded an OSCAR for 'Best Film' for <u>most years</u> between 1935 and 1976. The initials of each film and one of the main cast members are given to help you.   For Example:-

	1934	IHON	Clark Gable	*It Happened One Night*
1.	1935	MOTB	Charles Laughton	
2.	1939	GWTW	Clark Gable	
3.	1940	R	Laurence Olivier	
4.	1942	MM	Greer Garson	
5.	1943	C	Humphrey Bogart	
6.	1948	H	Laurence Olivier	
7.	1950	AAE	Bette Davis	
8.	1951	AAIP	Gene Kelly	
9.	1952	TGSOE	James Stewart	
10.	1953	FHTE	Burt Lancaster	
11.	1954	OTW	Marlon Brando	
12.	1955	M	Ernest Borgnine	
13.	1956	ATWI80D	David Niven	
14.	1957	TBOTRK	Alec Guinness	
15.	1958	G	Leslie Caron	
16.	1959	BH	Charlton Heston	
17.	1960	TA	Jack Lemmon	
18.	1961	WSS	Natalie Wood	
19.	1962	LOA	Peter O'Toole	
20.	1963	TJ	Albert Finney	
21.	1964	MFL	Rex Harrison	
22.	1965	TSOM	Julie Andrews	
23.	1966	AMFAS	Paul Scofield	
24.	1967	ITHOTN	Sidney Poitier	
25.	1968	O	Ron Moody	
26.	1969	MC	Dustin Hoffman	
27.	1970	P	George C. Scott	
28.	1971	TFC	Gene Hackman	
29.	1972	TG	Marlon Brando	
30.	1973	TS	Paul Newman	
31.	1974	TGP2	Al Pacino	
32.	1975	OFOTCN	Jack Nicholson	
33.	1976	R	Sylvester Stallone	

6. HALF TIME QUIZ TEAM NAME _____

You have to find the name of the film that was awarded an OSCAR for 'Best Film' in the given year. The initials of each film and one of the main cast members are given to help you.   For Example:-

| | 1977 | AH | Woody Allen | *Annie Hall* |

1.	1978	TDH	Robert De Nero	
2.	1979	KVK	Dustin Hoffman	
3.	1980	OP	Donald Sutherland	
4.	1981	COF	Ben Cross	
5.	1982	G	Ben Kingsley	
6.	1983	TOE	Shirley MacLaine	
7.	1984	A	Tom Hulce	
8.	1985	OOA	Meryl Streep	
9.	1986	P	Charlie Sheen	
10.	1987	TLE	Peter O'Toole	
11.	1988	RM	Dustin Hoffman	
12.	1989	DMD	Jessica Tandy	
13.	1990	DWW	Kevin Costner	
14.	1991	TSOTL	Anthony Hopkins	
15.	1992	U	Clint Eastwood	
16.	1993	SL	Liam Neeson	
17.	1994	FG	Tom Hanks	
18.	1995	B	Mel Gibson	
19.	1996	TEP	Ralph Fiennes	
20.	1997	T	Leonardo DiCaprio	
21.	1998	SIL	Gwyneth Paltrow	
22.	1999	AB	Kevin Spacey	
23.	2000	G	Russell Crowe	
24.	2001	ABM	Russell Crowe	
25.	2002	C	Renée Zellweger	
26.	2003	TLOTR:TROTK	Elijah Wood	
27.	2004	MDB	Clint Eastwood	
28.	2005	C	Sandra Bullock	
29.	2006	TD	Leonardo DiCaprio	
30.	2007	NCFOM	Tommy Lee Jones	
31.	2008	SM	Dev Patel	
32.	2009	THL	Jeremy Renner	
33.	2010	TKS	Colin Firth	

7. HALF TIME QUIZ TEAM NAME _____

The answers to all these questions are <u>one word film titles</u> (one answer is hyphenated). <u>None of them is preceded by the word 'The'</u>. To help you indentify the film you will be given the year it was released, one of its main stars and an extra piece of information which may be its genre or director. EXAMPLE:-

| | 1997 | Leonardo DiCaprio | Drama / Romance | *Titanic* |

	YEAR	STAR	INFORMATION	ANSWER
1.	1979	Sigourney Weaver	Horror / Sci Fi	A
2.	1988	Tom Hanks	Family comedy	B
3.	1995	Mel Gibson	Action / Drama	B
4.	1976	Sissy Spacek	Horror / Drama	C
5.	2002	Catherine Zeta-Jones	Musical / Drama	C
6.	1979	Laurence Olivier	Horror	D
7.	1960	Paul Newman	Historical Drama	E
8.	1980	Irene Cara	Musical	F
9.	1990	Patrick Swayze	Romance / Drama	G
10.	2000	Russell Crowe	Historical drama	G
11.	1948	Laurence Olivler	Classic drama	H
12.	2001	Judi Dench	Romantic biography	I
13.	1975	Roy Scheider	Thriller / Dir. Spielberg	J
14.	1969	Colin Welland	Drama / Dir. Ken Loach	K
15.	1970	Richard Attenborough	Crime comedy	L
16.	1927	Alfred Abel	Sci Fi / Silent / Dir. Fritz Lang	M
17.	1946	Cary Grant	Thriller / Dir. Hitchcock	N
18.	1955	Shirley Jones	Musical western	O
19.	1986	Charlie Sheen	War	P
20.	1973	Steve McQueen	Crime drama	P
21.	1979	Phil Daniels	Rock musical	Q
22.	1940	Laurence Olivier	Drama / Dir. Hitchcock	R
23.	1939	John Wayne	Western	S
24.	1960	Kirk Douglas	Action adventure	S
25.	1982	Dustin Hoffman	Comedy	T
26.	1992	Clint Eastwood	Western	U
27.	1958	James Stewart	Thriller / Dir. Hitchcock	V
28.	1995	Kevin Costner	Action adventure	W
29.	2000	Patrick Stewart	Sci Fi adventure	X
30.	1983	Barbara Streisand	Musical / Drama / Romance	Y
31.	1964	Stanley Baker	Action / War	Z

8. HALF TIME QUIZ   TEAM NAME _____

In the left column is the name of an animal that appeared in a film or TV programme (many are animated). All you have to do is name the type of animal it is. Vague answers such as bird or fish are not accepted.   ForExample:-

Elsa   Born Free   *Lion*

	Name of animal	Film	Type of animal
1.	Captain Flint	Treasure Island	
2.	Fly	Babe	
3.	Sebastian	The Little Mermaid	
4.	Hedwig	Harry Potter & The Chamber of Secrets	
5.	Willy	Free Willy	
6.	Colonel Hathi	The Jungle Book	
7.	Clyde	Every Which Way but Loose	
8.	Archimedes	The Sword in the Stone	
9.	Mumble	Happy Feet	
10.	Wilbur	Charlottes Web	
11.	Mij	Ring of Bright Water	
12.	Old Yeller	Old Yeller	
13.	Baby	Bringing up Baby	
14.	Nemo	Finding Nemo	
15.	Ben	Ben	
16.	Jemima	Miss Potter	
17.	Kehaar	Watership Down	
18.	Snowflake	Ace Ventura—Pet Detective	
19.	Marcel	Friends (TV)	
20.	Pumbaa	The Lion King	
21.	Polynesia	Dr Doolittle	
22.	Bernard	The Recuers	
23.	Mr Ed	Mr Ed (TV)	
24.	Snowbell	Stuart Little	
25.	Timothy	Dumbo	
26.	Manny	Ice Age	
27.	Flik	A Bugs Life	
28.	Lady	The Lady and the Tramp	
29.	Sam	The Muppet Show (TV)	
30.	Cheetah	Tarzan of the Apes	
31.	Dahl	Neighbours (TV)	
32.	Boxer	Animal Farm	

9. HALF TIME QUIZ TEAM NAME _____

Know your TV catchphrases !

Ex	What was Captain Mainwaring's put down, aimed at Private Pike ?	*You stupid boy*
1.	What did Alf Garnet frequently call his wife ?	
2.	'And now for something completely different' came from which TV show	
3.	'It's all done in the best possible taste!' came from whose show ?	
4.	Who was Catherine Tate's truculent teenager who was not bovvered ?	
5.	What did Roy Walker say when a contestant made a sensible but wrong guess ?	
6.	Who constantly wanted the door to be shut in a gameshow ?	
7.	In which game did you get nothing for a pair ?	
8.	' Can I have a P please Bob' ...... Which show ?	
9.	Which character was described as 'A dirty old man' by his son?	
10.	Which gameshow host said 'What is a hotspot not?' ?	
11.	What was Norman Stanley Fletcher's acceptable TV swearword ?	
12.	What was the BFH mentioned frequently by Jim Bowen in Bullseye ?	
13.	What did Mandy always say at the end of her sketch in Dick's show ?	
14.	Which actor played 'The only gay in the village' ?	
15.	In which show could you hear Richard say 'Start the fans please' ?	
16.	'Is it 'cos I is black' is said by whom when he is not allowed to do something	
17.	What must you not mention in a certain Torquay Hotel ?	
18.	What were the last words spoken in every episode of 'It Ain't Half Hot Mum'	
19.	Who said 'Pot as many balls as you can' ?	
20.	'We really want to see .... ' what, said Vic & Bob in their gameshow ?	
21.	Henry said 'You're playing catch up' in which show ?	
22.	Which character always said 'No-no-no-yes' when asked a question?	
23.	On which show did you hear 'Here's our Graham with a quick reminder'?	
24.	Baldrick always had a........ what, to get him out of trouble.	
25.	What did Ken & Kenneth frequently say to their customers ?	
26.	What did Michelle usually say when entering the cafe to see Rene ?	
27.	In which sit-com did CJ say 'I didn't get where I am today'	
28.	'Oh nice!' was uttered by which overweight character ?	

10. HALF TIME QUIZ TEAM NAME _____

	FILM	SONG
Ex.	The Sound of Music	*Climb Every Mountain*
1.	The Song of the South	
2.	The Wizard of Oz	
3.	Pinocchio	
4.	Me and My Girl	
5.	Calamity Jane	
6.	Singin' in the Rain	
7.	High Society	
8.	Oklahoma	
9.	Guys and Dolls	
10.	Carousel	
11.	The King and I	
12.	South Pacific	
13.	West Side Story	
14.	The Music Man	
15.	Summer Holiday	
16.	Fiddler on the Roof	
17.	My Fair Lady	
18.	Mary Poppins	
19.	The Jungle Book	
20.	Chitty Chitty Bang Bang	
21.	Cabaret	
22.	Oliver	
23.	Jesus Christ Superstar	
24.	Grease	
25.	Hair	
26.	The Lion King	
27.	Evita	
28.	Aladdin	
29.	The Phantom of the Opera	
30.	Moulin Rouge	
31.	Chicago	
32.	Mamma Mia	

An easy one ! Just match the songs below with the musical films on the left.

A Whole New World
America
Bachelor Boy
Climb Every Mountain
Consider Yourself
Ding-Dong the Witch is Dead
Feed the Birds
Give a Little Whistle
Good Morning Starshine
Hakuna Matata
Happy Talk
Hopelessly Devoted to You
I Could Have Danced All Night
I Don't Know how to Love Him
If I were a Rich Man
Like a Virgin
Make 'em Laugh
March of the Siamese Children
Me Ol' Bamboo
Oh What a Beautiful Morning
Oh What a Circus
Our Last Summer
Razzle Dazzle
Secret Love
Seventy-Six Trombones
Sit Down You're Rocking the Boat
The Bare Necessities
The Lambeth Walk
The Music of the Night
Willkommen
Who Wants to be a Millionaire
You'll Never Walk Alone
Zip-a-Dee-Doo-Dah

11. HALF TIME QUIZ   TEAM NAME_____

Walt Disney's classic animated cartoon films have given way to Pixar's computer generated films more recently. All you have to do is work out which Disney classic films the following characters come from. They are not in any particular order.

	Character	Film
Ex.	Tod	*The Fox and the Hounds*
1.	Alan-a-Dale	
2.	Thomas O'Malley	
3.	Belle	
4.	John Smith	
5.	Sebastian	
6.	Perdita	
7.	Fairy Godmother	
8.	Flora the Pink Fairy	
9.	Zazu	
10.	The Magic Mirror	
11.	Esmeralda	
12.	Mister Gepetto	
13.	Queen of Hearts	
14.	Timothy Mouse	
15.	Kaa	
16.	The Sorcerer's Apprentice	
17.	Princess Jasmine	
18.	Archimedes	
19.	Tiger Lily	
20.	Captain Li Shang	
21.	Flower	
22.	Si and Am	
23.	Zeus and Hera	
24.	Bernard	
25.	Owl	

12. HALF TIME QUIZ TEAM NAME _____

These are all famous lines from well known films. Name the film.

1.	1971	"You've got to ask yourself one question: 'Do I feel lucky?' Well, do ya, punk?"	
2.	1987	"Nobody puts 'Baby' in a corner."	
3.	1970	"Love means never having to say you're sorry".	
4.	1942	"Here's looking at you, kid".	
5.	1940	"Last night, I dreamt I went to Manderley again...We can never go back to Manderley again. That much is certain".	
6.	1994	"Mama always said life was like a box of chocolates. You never know what you're gonna get."	
7.	2003	She's all set to marry Norrington just like she promised and you get to die for her just like you promised, so we're all men of our word really, except for Elizabeth who is in fact a woman.	
8.	1950	"Fasten your seatbelts. It's going to be a bumpy night."	
9.	1980	"Here's Johnny"	
10.	1939	"Frankly, my dear. I don't give a damn".	
11.	1952	"What do they think I am? Dumb or something? Why, I make more money than - than, than Calvin Coolidge! Put together!"	
12.	1964	"She's so deliciously low. So horribly dirty".	
13.	1967	"We rob banks"	
14.	1997	"Just the other night I was sleeping under a bridge, and now here I am, on the grandest ship in the world, having champagne with you fine people".	
15.	1954	"You don't understand! I coulda had class. I coulda been a contender. I could've been somebody, instead of a bum, which is what I am."	
16.	1989	"I'll have what she's having."	
17.	1935	"You can't fool me! There ain't no sanity clause!"	
18.	1964	"Gentlemen, you can't fight in here! This is the War Room".	
19.	1972	"I'm going to make him an offer he can't refuse."	
20.	1999	"I'm also just a girl standing in front of a boy asking him to love her."	
21.	1933	"Oh, no, it wasn't the airplanes. It was Beauty killed the Beast."	
22.	1991	"Hasta la vista, baby".	
23.	2003	"Fish are friends, not food".	
24.	1939	"I'll get you, my pretty, and your little dog too"	
25.	1977	"You must repair him! Sir, if any of my circuits or gears will help, I'll gladly donate them".	
26.	1979	"This is Ripley, last survivor of the *Nostromo*, signing off. "	

13. HALF TIME QUIZ   TEAM NAME _____

All the James Bond movies have had a title song or theme associated with them.
The films (including two unofficial ones) are listed below and all you have to do is
match the singer in the box on the right with the correct film. Watch out though,
not all the songs have the same title as the film it comes from, though the title
doesn't matter here and at least one singer has to be used more than once.

Ex.	Dr No	*John Barry Orchestra*
1.	**From Russia with Love**	
2.	**Goldfinger**	
3.	**Thunderball**	
4.	**You Only Live Twice**	
5.	**On Her Majesty's Secret Service**	
6.	**Diamonds are Forever**	
7.	**Live and let Die**	
8.	**The Man With the Golden Gun**	
9.	**The Spy Who Loved Me**	
10.	**Moonraker**	
11.	**For Your Eyes Only**	
12.	**Octopussy**	
13.	**A View to a Kill**	
14.	**The Living Daylights**	
15.	**License to Kill**	
16.	**Goldeneye**	
17.	**Tomorrow Never Dies**	
18.	**The World is not Enough**	
19.	**Die Another Day**	
20.	**Casino Royale (2006)**	
21.	**Quantum of Solace**	
22.	**Skyfall**	
	UNOFFICIAL BOND FILMS	###################
23.	**Casino Royale (1967)**	
24.	**Never Say Never Again**	

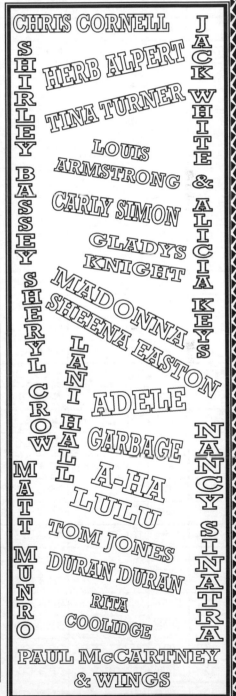

CHRIS CORNELL
SHIRLEY BASSEY
HERB ALPERT
JACK WHITE & ALICIA KEYS
TINA TURNER
LOUIS ARMSTRONG
CARLY SIMON
GLADYS KNIGHT
MADONNA
SHEENA EASTON
SHERYL CROW
LANI HALL
ADELE
GARBAGE
A-HA
LULU
NANCY SINATRA
MATT MUNRO
TOM JONES
DURAN DURAN
RITA COOLIDGE
PAUL McCARTNEY & WINGS

14. HALF TIME QUIZ TEAM NAME _____

	YEAR	FILM	ACTORS	FILM (ANSWER)
Ex.	1997	T	LD'C & KW	*Titanic*
1.	1935	TH	FA & GR	
2.	1938	BUB	CG & KH	
3.	1939	GWTW	CG & VL	
4.	1940	R	LO & JF	
5.	1942	C	HB & IB	
6.	1945	BE	TH & CJ	
7.	1949	AR	ST & KH	
8.	1950	SB	WH & GS	
9.	1952	SITR	GK & DR	
10.	1952	HN	GC & GK	
11.	1953	FHTE	BL & DK	
12.	1955	RWAC	JD & NW	
13.	1960	P	AP & JL	
14.	1961	BAT	GP & AH	
15.	1963	MOD	JG & DD	
16.	1964	VLV	EP & AM	
17.	1965	DZ	OS & JC	
18.	1967	TG	DH & AB	
19.	1967	BAC	WB & FD	
20.	1977	AH	WA & DK	
21.	1981	TFLW	JI & MS	
22.	1987	FA	MD & GC	
23.	1988	AFCW	JC & JLC	
24.	1990	G	PS & DM	
25.	1990	PW	RG & JR	
26.	1991	TSOTL	AH & JF	
27.	1992	BI	MD & SS	
28.	1993	SIS	TH & MR	
29.	2001	MR	EMG & NK	
30.	2003	LIT	BM & SJ	
31.	2007	HPATOOTP	DR & EW	
32.	2008	TCCOBB	BP & CB	
33.	2010	TKS	CF & HBC	

The following initials stand for reasonably well known films in the given years. The next column gives the initials of the principal male and female actors (in that order). All you have to do is identify the film but not the actors.

15. HALF TIME QUIZ TEAM NAME _____

You have to write down the type of place, building, transport or institution that most, (sometimes all), of the following films are set in.   For example:-

Murder on the Orient Express	*A train*
The Great Escape	*A German prisoner of War camp*
In Which We Serve	*A Naval ship*

1.	How to Steal a Million	
2.	The Shining	
3.	Twelve Angry Men	
4.	Casablanca	
5.	Papillon	
6.	The Memphis Belle	
7.	MASH	
8.	Goodbye Mr Chips	
9.	Brief Encounter	
10.	Empire of the Sun	
11.	Dog Day Afternoon	
12.	The Poseidon Adventure	
13.	Seven Brides for Seven Brothers	
14.	Fantastic Voyage	
15.	One Flew Over the Cuckoo's Nest	
16.	Summer Holiday	
17.	The Lady Vanishes	
18.	The Cruel Sea	
19.	Chicago	
20.	The Magnificent Seven	
21.	Key Largo	
22.	Judgement at Nuremberg	
23.	Black Swan	
24.	Schlindler's List	
25.	The King and I	
26.	The African Queen	
27.	Psycho	
28.	Grease	
29.	Love Story	
30.	Tootsie	
31.	Alien	

16. HALF TIME QUIZ   TEAM NAME _____

The popular Christmas songs in this list were recorded by the singers in the list on the right. Match the singer to the song recorded in the given year.

1.	1942	White Christmas	
2.	1944	Have Yourself a Merry Little Christmas	
3.	1947	All I want for Christmas is My Two Front Teeth	
4.	1949	Rudolf the Red Nosed Reindeer	
5.	1951	It's Beginning to Look Like Christmas	
6.	1953	Santa Baby	
7.	1957	Blue Christmas	
8.	1958	Rockin' Around the Christmas Tree	
9.	1959	Let it Snow Let it Snow Let it Snow	
10.	1963	The Christmas Song	
11.	1963	The Most Wonderful Time of the Year	
12.	1971	Happy Christmas, War is Over	
13.	1973	I Wish it Could be Christmas Every Day	
14.	1973	Step into Christmas	
15.	1973	Merry Christmas Everybody	
16.	1974	Lonely This Christmas	
17.	1975	A Spaceman Came Travelling	
18.	1975	In Dulce Jubilo	
19.	1975	I Believe in Father Christmas	
20.	1977	Peace on Earth	
21.	1979	Wonderful Christmas Time	
22.	1980	Stop the Cavalry	
23.	1981	Christmas Wrapping	
24.	1984	Little Saint Nick	
25.	1984	Last Christmas	
26.	1984	Do They Know it's Christmas	
27.	1985	Walking in the Air	
28.	1987	Fairy Tale of New York	
29.	1988	Driving Home for Christmas	
30.	1988	Mistletoe and Wine	
31.	1994	All I Want for Christmas is You	

Gene Autry
Band Aid
Mariah Carey
Nat King Cole
Perry Como
The Beach Boys
Bing Crosby & David Bowie
Bing Crosby
Chris De Burgh
Judy Garland
Elton John
John & Yoko
Spike Jones
Aled Jones
Eartha Kitt
Greg Lake
Brenda Lee
Jona Lewie
Dean Martin
Paul McCartney
Mud
Mike Oldfield
Pogues & Kirsty McColl
Elvis Presley
Chris Rea
Cliff Richard
Slade
The Waitresses
Wham
Andy Williams
Wizzard

17. HALF TIME QUIZ   TEAM NAME _____

You have to identify the countries of birth of all the people in the following list. **NOTE None of them were born in the UK or USA.**

Ex.	Cliff Richard (singer)	*India*
1.	Ursula Andress (Actress, first 'Bond' girl)	
2.	Irving Berlin (Composer & Lyricist)	
3.	Justin Bieber (Singer & Actor)	
4.	Cate Blanchett (Actress)	
5.	Pierce Brosnon (Actor)	
6.	Jim Carrey (Actor)	
7.	Frank Capra (Film Director)	
8.	Russell Crowe (Actor)	
9.	Penelope Cruz (Actress)	
10.	Gloria Estefan (Singer)	
11.	Che Guevara (Revolutionary Leader)	
12.	Audrey Hepburn (Actress)	
13.	Rachel Hunter (Supermodel)	
14.	Grace Jones (Singer & Actress)	
15.	Eddie Jordan (Owner of 'Jordan Grand Prix')	
16.	Katie Melua (Singer)	
17.	Freddie Mercury (Lead singer with 'Queen')	
18.	Spike Milligan (Comedian & Writer)	
19.	Rupert Murdoch (Owner of 'News International')	
20.	Greg Norman (Golfer)	
21.	Theo Paphitis (Dragon's Den)	
22.	Kevin Pieterson (Cricketer)	
23.	Rihanna (Singer)	
24.	Cristiano Ronaldo (Footballer)	
25.	Arnold Schwarzenegger (Actor)	
26.	Omar Sharif (Actor)	
27.	Sandi Toksvig (Actress, Comedienne, TV Presenter)	
28.	J R R Tolkien (Author)	
29.	Emma Watson (Actress)	
30.	Bradley Wiggins (Winner of 'Tour de France')	
31.	Bruce Willis (Actor)	

18. HALF TIME QUIZ   TEAM NAME _____

This quiz is all about film remakes. For each question you will be given the years of the films and initials of the title plus some other information.   **EXAMPLE:—**

| | ACC | 1984 | Dickens story. Starring George C Scott | *A Christmas Carol* |
| | | 1999 | Starring Patrick Stewart | |

No.	Initials	Year	Information	Answer
1.	TFOTP	1965 2004	Aviation story. Starring James Stewart Starring Dennis Quaid	
2.	TF	1958 1986	Sc Fi horror. Starring David Hedison Starring Jeff Goldblum & Geena Davis	
3.	KK	1933 2005	Classic. Starring Fay Wray Starring Naomi Watts	
4.	TLV	1938 1979	Hitchcock. Starring Margaret Lockwood. Starring Elliott Gould & Cybil Shepherd	
5.	POTA	1968 2001	Sci fi. Starring Charlton Heston Starring Mark Wahlberg	
6.	101D	1961 1996	Disney animation Starring Glenn Close	
7.	TNP	1963 1996	Comedy. Starring Jerry Lewis Starring Eddie Murphy	
8.	TTNS	1935 1978	Thriller. Starring Robert Donat Starring Robert Powell	
9.	TG	1969 2010	Western. Starring John Wayne Starring Jeff Bridges	
10.	SD	1971 2011	Thriller. Starring Dustin Hoffman Starring James Marsden	
11.	TPT	1961 1998	Children's film. Starring Hayley Mills Starring Lindsay Lohan	
12.	TIJ	1969 2003	Crime thriller. Starring Michael Caine Starring Donald Sutherland	
13.	TDTESS	1951 2008	Sc fi. Starring Michael Rennie Starring Keanu Reeves	
14.	ANOES	1984 2010	Horror. Starring Johnny Depp Starring Jack Earle Haley	
15.	OE	1960 2001	Crime thriller. Starring Frank Sinatra Starring George Clooney & Brad Pitt	
16.	TTCA	1968 1999	Romantic thriller. Starring Steve McQueen Starring Pierce Brosnan & Rene Russo	
17.	P	1960 1998	Horror thriller. Starring Anthony Perkins Starring Vince Vaughan & Julianne Moore	
18.	AIW	1951 2010	Children's classic. Disney animation. Disney remake . Starring Johnny Depp (voice)	
19.	A	1966 2004	Romantic comedy. Starring Michael Caine Starring Jude Law	
20.	TPA	1972 2005	Disaster film. Starring Gene Hackman Starring Adam Baldwin & Rutger Hauer	
21.	CR	1967 2006	Action adventure. Starring David Niven Starring Daniel Craig	

19. HALF TIME QUIZ   TEAM NAME _____

This is one that needs contributions from people of all ages. On the table below are the initials of some songs and artistes for four number 1 hits from each of the years ending in a '0' from 1960 onwards. All you have to do is identify them.

	Year	Song	Singer	Song Title	Singer(s)
Example(2010) GT		RD		*Good Times*	*Roll Deep*
1.	1960	CC	TEB		
2.	1960	INON	EP		
3.	1960	A	TS		
4.	1960	MOMAD	LD		
5.	1970	ITS	MJ		
6.	1970	WS	LM		
7.	1970	BOTW	S & G		
8.	1970	BOG	FP		
9.	1980	DSSCTM	TP		
10.	1980	NOQLG	SWSC		
11.	1980	ST	A		
12.	1980	TTIH	B		
13.	1990	V	M		
14.	1990	ALT	TBS		
15.	1990	SD	CR		
16.	1990	IIB	VI		
17.	2000	B	TC		
18.	2000	LIAR	RK		
19.	2000	OIDIA	BS		
20.	2000	CWFI	BTB		
21.	2010	H	TXFF		
22.	2010	BR	LG		
23.	2010	WWC	MC		
24.	2010	CG	KP & SD		

Source — '1000 Number Ones' by Jon Kutner & Spencer Leigh & 'Number-Ones' website

20. HALF TIME QUIZ   TEAM NAME _____

This is one that needs contributions from people of all ages. On the table below are the initials of some songs and artistes for four number 1 hits from each of the years ending in a '3' from 1953 to 2003. All you have to do is identify them.

Example(1963) SFMS	TS	*Sweets for my Sweet*	*The Searchers*

	Year	Song	Singer	Song Title	Singer(s)
1.	1953	IB	FL		
2.	1953	SWRF	GM		
3.	1953	AM	DW		
4.	1953	HMIDITW	LR		
5.	1963	FMTY	TB		
6.	1963	DID	EP		
7.	1963	ILI	G&TP		
8.	1963	TWW	FI		
9.	1973	B	S		
10.	1973	CTC	SQ		
11.	1973	TTON	DO		
12.	1973	GD	GO'S		
13.	1983	UG	BJ		
14.	1983	OY	FP		
15.	1983	WILMH	PY		
16.	1983	KC	CC		
17.	1993	IDAFL	ML		
18.	1993	P	TT		
19.	1993	YAH	TB		
20.	1993	MB	MB		
21.	2003	LRN	WY		
22.	2003	WITL	BEP		
23.	2003	M	W		
24.	2003	SITS	GG&TK		

Source — '1000 Number Ones' by Jon Kutner & Spencer

21. HALF TIME QUIZ TEAM NAME_____

This is one that needs contributions from people of all ages. On the table below are the initials of the songs and artistes for four number 1 hits from each of the years ending in a '4' from 1954 onwards. All you have to do is

Example(1954) SAN	JR	*Such A Night*	*Johnny Ray*

	Year	Song	Singer	Song Title	Singer(s)
1.	1954	SL	DD		
2.	1954	CM	DW		
3.	1954	TCIAF	FS		
4.	1954	OMP	EC		
5.	1964	THOTRS	TA		
6.	1964	IFF	TB		
7.	1964	IISG	HH		
8.	1964	HITR	TH		
9.	1974	S	CA		
10.	1974	LMFAR	TO		
11.	1974	GMYAS	DE		
12.	1974	SBL	TR		
13.	1984	IJCTSILY	SW		
14.	1984	TPOL	FGTH		
15.	1984	F	W		
16.	1984	DTKIC	BA		
17.	1994	LIAA	WWW		
18.	1994	SN	W		
19.	1994	WY	MC		
20.	1994	EC	TT		
21.	2004	R	RW		
22.	2004	ISBY	GA		
23.	2004	JLI	E		
24.	2004	MG	PA		

Source — '1000 Number Ones' by Jon Kutner & Spencer

22. HALF TIME QUIZ TEAM NAME_____

The UK music charts started in 1952. Since then there have been over 1000 number 1 hits. All you have to do is to indentify the song from the clue and initials, and the singer(s) or performers. The year is given to help you. For example:-

| First number 1 ever | 1952 | HIMH | *Here In My Heart* | *Al Martino* |

	CLUE	YEAR	INITIALS	SONG	SINGER(S)
1.	Longest time at number 1 (18 weeks , not continuous)	1953	IB		
2.	Only song to have topped the charts 4 times with 4 different singers.	1955	UM		(First singer only)
3.	First single to enter the UK charts at number 1	1960	MOM AD		
4.	First single to sell a million copies in the UK	1963	SLY		
5.	Unexpected top selling single of 1965	1965	T		
6.	Longest single at 7 minutes 20 seconds	1968	M-AP		
7.	First single to sell 2 million copies in the UK alone	1977	MOK		
8.	Only German Eurovision song contest winner ever. Number 1 all over Europe including the UK	1982	ALP		
9.	Charity single to raise money for Bradford City FC after the fire	1985	YNW A		
10.	Longest continuous run at number 1, 16 weeks	1991	ETID		
11.	Up to 1996 the biggest selling single by a female group, (UK)	1996	W		
12.	Greatest selling single ever in the World	1997	CITW		
13.	Oscar winning song, the first to enter the UK & US charts at number 1 by a female singer	1998	MHW GO		
14.	Oldest female singer to top the charts at 52	1998	B		
15.	First fictional character to reach number 1 twice (first hit).	2000	CWFI		
16.	1000th number 1 (20th number 1 for this singer)	2005	ON		

Source—1000 UK Number One Hits by John Cutner & Spencer Leigh

23. HALF TIME QUIZ TEAM NAME _____

The following singers have all recorded, and had hits with, songs from musical films or stage plays. Some are cover versions and some are the original singers in the film or stage production. The singer, musical and year are given, all you have to do is write down the title of the song.

1.	Bing Crosby	1942	Holiday Inn	
2.	Bing Crosby & Grace Kelly	1956	High Society	
3.	Vic Damone	1958	My Fair Lady	
4.	Shirley Bassey	1960	Oliver	
5.	The Beatles	1963	The Music Man	
6.	Harry Secombe	1963	Pickwick	
7.	Gerry & The Pacemakers	1963	Carousel	
8.	Rolf Harris	1967	Fiddler on the Roof	
9.	Vince Hill	1967	The Sound of Music	
10.	Shirley Bassey	1967	Sweet Charity	
11.	The Nice	1968	West Side Story	
12.	5th Dimension	1969	Hair	
13.	Helen Reddy	1971	Jesus Christ Superstar	
14.	Liza Minnelli	1975	Chicago	
15.	Judy Covington	1976	Evita	
16.	Olivia Newton-John	1978	Grease	
17.	John Travolta & Olivia Newton-John	1978	Grease	
18.	Elaine Paige	1981	Cats	
19.	Captain Sensible	1982	South Pacific	
20.	Cliff Richard & Sarah Brightman	1986	Phantom of the Opera	
21.	Michael Ball	1989	Aspects of Love	
22.	Eva Cassidy	1992	The Wizard of Oz	
23.	Elton John	1994	The Lion King	
24.	Pet Shop Boys	1997	West Side Story	
25.	Boyzone	1998	Whistle Down the Wind	

24. HALF TIME QUIZ TEAM NAME _____

Below are listed 25 'novelty songs' from the last 50 years. Some are good old favourites, (from the Uncle Mac days), others are just plain annoying, these are the ones you wish had never been made. Most have been in the top 20, some at number 1. All you have to do is match the name from the box with the song. They are not in any particular order.

Ex.	Tie me Kangaroo Down Sport	*Rolf Harris*
1.	**Shuddup Your Face**	
2.	Hello Muddah Hello Faddah	
3.	**Snoopy Vs The Red Baron**	
4.	**My Ding-a-ling**	
5.	**Convoy**	
6.	**Ernie**	
7.	**My Old Man's a Dustman**	
8.	**Speedy Gonzales**	
9.	**The Banana Boat Song**	
10.	**Monster Mash**	
11.	**Axel F**	
12.	**Hole in the Ground**	
13.	**Lily the Pink**	
14.	How much is that doggie in the window	
15.	They're coming to take me away	
16.	**My Brother**	
17.	**The Hippopotamus Song**	
18.	**The Chicken Song**	
19.	**The Lumberjack Song**	
20.	**Yellow Polka-Dot Bikini**	
21.	**A Hard Days Night**	
22.	**Purple People Eater**	
23.	**Three Little Fishes**	
24.	**The Streak**	
25.	My Boomerang won't come back	

BRIAN HYLAND
TERRY SCOTT
LITA ROZA
BENNY HILL
PAT BOONE
FRANKIE HOWARD
THE SCAFFOLD
BOBBY PICKETT
FLANDERS & SWANN
NAPOLEON XIV
LONNIE DONEGAN
SPITTING IMAGE
MONTY PYTHON
JOE DOLCE
ALLAN SHERMAN
CHARLIE DRAKE
HARRY BELAFONTE
CHUCK BERRY
C W McCALL
PETER SELLERS
BERNARD CRIBBINS
RAY STEVENS
SHEB WOOLEY
CRAZY FROG
ROYAL GUARDSMEN

25. HALF TIME QUIZ   TEAM NAME _____

The following artistes all had instrumental hit records in the year given. Can you name the hits, the initials are given to help you.?

	YEAR	ARTISTE	INITIALS	HIT RECORD
1.	1954	Eddie Calvert	OMP	
2.	1955	Perez Prado	CPAABW	
3.	1956	Winifred Atwell	PPOP	
4.	1958	Lord Rockingham's XI	HM	
5.	1959	Russ Conway	SS	
6.	1960	Bert Kaempfert & his Orchestra	WBN	
7.	1960	The Shadows	A	
8.	1961	Henry Mancini's Orchestra	MR	
9.	1961	Dave Brubeck Quartet	TF	
10.	1962	David Rose & His Orchestra	TS	
11.	1962	Mr Acker Bilk	SOTS	
12.	1962	Kenny Ball and his Jazzmen	MIM	
13.	1962	The Shadows	WL	
14.	1962	The Tornados	T	
15.	1962	B Bumble & the Stingers	NR	
16.	1962	Booker T & the MGs	GO	
17.	1963	The Surfaris	WO	
18.	1965	Horst Jankowski	AWITBF	
19.	1965	Sounds Orchestral	CYFTTW	
20.	1965	Marcello Minerbi	ZD	
21.	1966	Herb Alpert & the Tijuana Brass	SF	
22.	1967	Whistling Jack Smith	IWKBB	
23.	1968	Hugo Montenegro	TGTBATU	
24.	1968	Mason Williams	CG	
25.	1969	Fleetwood Mac	A	
26.	1972	Lieutenant Pigeon	MOD	
27.	1972	Royal Scots Dragoon Guards	AG	
28.	1972	Hot Butter	P	
29.	1973	Marvin Hamlisch	TE	
30.	1973	The Simon Park Orchestra	EL	
31.	1977	The Brighouse & Rastrick Band	TFD	
32.	1982	Vangelis	COF	

26. HALF TIME QUIZ   TEAM NAME _____

This quiz sheet is all about five well known singers, there will be five questions on each of them.   They are:-
FRANK SINATRA,   ELVIS PRESLEY,   SHIRLEY BASSEY,   TOM JONES   &   MADONNA

	FRANK SINATRA	##################
1.	He was born in Hoboken in 1915 in which US state?	
2.	To which film actress was he married from 1951 to 1957?	
3.	In which film did he appear in 1956 with Grace Kelly and Bing Crosby?	
4.	Which record label did he establish in the 1960s?	
5.	Which song did Paul Anka write especially for him in the 1960s?	
	ELVIS PRESLEY	##################
6.	In which year was he born ?	
7.	With which record company did he record from 1953 to 55 ?	
8.	What was his first US number 1 with RCA Victor in 1956 ?	
9.	Which Elvis song, recorded in 1968, didn't become a worldwide hit until 2002 ?	
10.	What was the name of his only child who was born in 1968?	
	SHIRLEY BASSEY	##################
11.	In which city was she born in 1937?	
12.	With which song, from the musical 'Sweet Charity', did she have a hit ?	
13.	As well as 'Goldfinger' and 'Diamonds are For Ever' which other 'Bond' song did she sing?	
14.	With which British/Australian film star did she have an affair in the 60s?	
15.	At which major UK event did she perform in 2012 ?	
	TOM JONES	##################
16.	Tom Jones was a Welsh miner before becoming a singer. True or False?	
17.	Which song from 'The Full Monty' did he sing?	
18.	Which 'Bond' song did he sing?	
19.	How many times has he been married?	
20.	Which honour did he receive in 1995 before his knighthood in 2005?	
	MADONNA	##################
21.	Which Madonna hit was sung by two men in the 2001 film 'Moulin Rouge' ?	
22.	In which Lloyd-Webber & Rice musical film did she play a leading role?	
23.	Which song did she record for the film 'The Spy Who Shagged Me'	
24.	Who did she marry at Skibo Castle in Scotland in 2000 ?	
25.	From which African country did she adopt a orphan boy in 2008 ?	

27. HALF TIME QUIZ   TEAM NAME _____

For each question there are two lines of the lyrics from a well known song. The songs are very varied including, classic pop songs, wartime songs, and old English songs such as sung at the 'Last Night of the Proms'. All you have to do is identify the songs.

	LYRICS	SONG
1.	'And Jimmy Will go to Sleep In His Own Little Room Again'	
2.	'Don't Tell Me it's Not Worth Fighting For I Can't Help it -There's Nothing I Want More'	
3.	'Thy Choicest Gifts in Store On Her be Pleased to Pour'	
4.	'Paddy wrote a Letter to His Irish Molly O Saying "Should You Not Receive it, Write and let Me Know!"'	
5.	'At the End of the Storm is a Golden Sky And the Sweet Silver Song of a Lark'	
6.	'She Tied You to her Kitchen Chair She Broke Your Throne and She Cut Your Hair'	
7.	'They'll be Happy to Know that as I Saw You go You were Singing This Song'	
8.	'Swift to its Close Ebbs out Life's Little Day Earth's Joys Grow Dim, its Glories Pass Away'	
9.	'Sail on Silver Girl, Sail on by Your Time has Come to Shine'	
10.	'And did the Continence Divine Shine Forth Upon Our Clouded Hills'	
11.	'I Hope Someday You'll Join us And the World Will be as One'	
12.	'He's Just a Poor Boy From a Poor Family Spare Him His Life From this Monstrosity'	
13.	'Yes There were Times, I'm Sure You Knew When I Bit off More Than I Could Chew'	
14.	'Where the Treetops Glisten And Children Listen'	
15.	'Truth and Right and Freedom, each Holy Gem Stars of Solemn Brightness, Weave Thy Diadem'	
16.	'This Was the Charter, the Charter of the Land And Guardian Angels Sang this Strain'	
17.	'Now You Belong to Heaven And Stars Spell out Your Name'	
18.	'The Lights are Much Brighter There You Can Forget all Your Troubles, Forget all Your Cares'	
19.	'Anybody Could be that Guy Night is Young and the Music's High'	

28. HALF TIME QUIZ   TEAM NAME _____

These are the <u>opening lyrics</u> to well known pop songs. They come from 5 different decades. Can you identify the songs, all were UK number 1s.

	SIXTIES	##############
1.	Trailers for sale or rent. Rooms to let fifty cents.	
2.	I thought love was only true in fairy tales.	
3.	You keep saying you've got something for me, something you call love. But confess.	
4.	Dirty old river, must you keep rolling. Flowing into the night.	
5.	Love love love love love love love love love. There's nothing you can do that can't be done. Nothing you can sing that can't be sung.	
	SEVENTIES	###############
6.	You fill up my senses. Like a night in a forest.	
7.	Sometimes it's hard to be a woman. Giving all your love to just one man	
8.	I've been cheated by you since I don't know when.	
9.	It won't be easy, you'll think it's strange, when I try to explain how I feel. That I still need your love after all that I've done.	
10.	Girl when you hold me. How you control me. You bend and you fold me.	
	EIGHTIES	###############
11.	Calling out around the World. Are you ready for a brand new beat	
12.	You've gotta speed it up. And then you've gotta slow it down.	
13.	She was more like a beauty queen from a movie scene.	
14.	There's a loving in your eyes all the way. If I listened to your lies would you say. I'm a man without conviction.	
15.	I feel so unsure. As I take you by the hand and lead you to the dance floor.	
	NINETIES	###############
16.	Look into my eyes, you will see. What you mean to me.	
17.	If I should stay. I would only be in your way. So I'll go but I know.	
18.	I feel it in my fingers. I feel it in my toes.	
19.	Baby if you've got to go away. I don't think I can take the pain	
20.	Yo, I'll tell you what I want, what I really really want	
	TWO THOUSANDS	###############
21.	I think I did it again. I made you believe. We're more than just friends.	
22.	Me with the floorshow. Kickin' with your torso. Boys getting high.	
23.	Humidity's rising. Barometer's getting low.	
24.	I'm here just like I said. Though it's breaking every rule I've ever made. My racing heart is just the same. Why make it strong to break it once again.	
25.	When I am down and, oh my soul, so weary. When troubles come and my heart burdened be. Then I am still and wait here in the silence.	

29. HALF TIME QUIZ   TEAM NAME _____

All these questions are to do with various adverts. Where a question refers to a product, the brand name should be included in your answer. Eg. If a question was about tea, you would have to include the brand name as well.

1.	What was 'A lot less bovver than a hover' ?	
2.	'Does she or doesn't she ?' — do what with what in 1964	
3.	'Out of the strong came forth sweetness' - which product?	
4.	Which characters were created in the 1930s for Kelloggs	
5.	Which TV 'veteran' advertises AXA Sun Life Insurance ?	
6.	Which company uses "Ghostbusters" and "Eye of a Tiger" among other songs for their adverts ?	
7.	Where did 'Your fingers do the walking' ?	
8.	Which product was advertised by a romantic story built up over several adverts, in the 80s and 90s.	
9.	Which advert featured the song "She's Always a Woman" ?	
10.	What company used 'The appliance of science' ?	
11.	What must you not leave home without (in 1975) ?	
12.	Which cigarette were you never alone with in the 60s	
13.	What was 'Finger lickin' good' ?	
14.	What gave you the 'Ring of confidence' in the 1960s ?	
15.	What product used 'Milk from contented cows' ?	
16.	The slogan 'It is. Are you?' was for which newspaper in 1987 ?	
17.	For what type of beer was 'Your right arm for' ?	
18.	Joanna Lumley advertises for which insurance company?	
19.	Which Hollywood legend advertised sherry in the 60s.	
20.	What is the best selling book by Aleksandr Orlov called ?	
21.	'Wotalotlgot !' A lot of what in 1961 ?	
22.	What was soft, strong and very long ?	

30. HALF TIME QUIZ TEAM NAME _____

WELL KNOWN PEOPLE WHO DIED IN **2011.** All you have to do is work out who died in 2011 from their initials, their gender, their age and a clue.

	Initials	Sex	Age	Famous for:-	Name
1.	SB	M	54	Golfer	
2.	TB	M	76	Comedy actor (Are You Being Served)	
3.	JB	M	77	Film theme composer (Bond)	
4.	OBL	M	54	Terrorist leader	
5.	JB	F	87	Impressionist entertainer	
6.	HC	M	76	British boxer	
7.	DC	M	89	TV Sit-com writer (Dad's Army)	
8.	BD	F	91	Soap actress (Coronation Street)	
9.	PF	M	83	American actor (Detective)	
10.	BF	F	93	Former 'First Lady'	
11.	JF	M	67	American boxer	
12.	MG	M	69	African dictator	
13.	JH	M	71	Bass guitarist with a 60s group	
14.	SJ	M	56	Computer entrepreneur	
15.	KJ-i	M	70	Dictator	
16.	DK-S	M	88	Children's author	
17.	TL	M	90	Snooker commentator	
18.	GM	M	48	British Boxer	
19.	GMcC	M	80	Racehorse trainer	
20.	PP	M	64	British actor	
21.	GR	M	63	Singer / songwriter	
22.	CR	M	88	American film actor	
23.	JR	F	89	American film actress	
24.	KR	M	84	Film director	
25.	JS	M	85	DJ & TV presenter (now disgraced)	
26.	GS	M	42	Football manager (Wales)	
27.	ES	M	56	Haulage magnate	
28.	ET	F	79	Actress	
29.	AW	F	27	Singer / songwriter	
30.	SY	F	72	British actress	

31. HALF TIME QUIZ TEAM NAME_____

All you have to do is answer the following questions about music or song writers.

1.	Who wrote 'Claire de lune'?	
2.	Who wrote the music for 'Rule Britannia'?	
3.	Who wrote 'The Blue Danube?	
4.	Who wrote 'The Liberty Bell', (Monty Python theme)?	
5.	Which singer wrote 'My Way' especially for Frank Sinatra?	
6.	Who wrote the music for the Oscar winning film 'West Side Story'?	
7.	Who wrote the music for 'Oklahoma', 'South Pacific' and 'The Sound of Music'?	
8.	Which one wrote the music, George or Ira Gershwin?	
9.	Who wrote Bing Crosby's 'White Christmas'?	
10.	Who wrote the music for Petula Clark's 'Downtown' and the theme tune for 'Neighbours'?	
	Of the following 4 pairs, which one wrote the music?	###################
11.	Lerner & Lowe	
12.	Bacharach & David	
13.	Lloyd-Webber & Rice	
14.	Goffin & King	
15.	Who wrote the music for 'The Lion King'?	
16.	Which 'Country & Western' singer wrote Witney Houston's 'I will always love you'?	
17.	True or False—Gene Kelly wrote 'Singin' in the Rain'	
18.	T or F—The Beatles only sung Lennon & McCartney songs.	
19.	T or F — Comedian Frank Skinner co-wrote the football song 'Three lions' for 'Euro 96'	
20.	Who wrote 'The Mighty Quinn', 'With God on our Side' and 'Just like a Woman' all sung by Manfred Mann?	
21.	Complete this song writing team 'Holland, Dozier & ....'	
22.	Which member of 'Take That' writes many of their songs?	
23.	Who wrote 'Hallelujah', that was covered by Alexandra Burke in 2008?	

32. HALF TIME QUIZ   TEAM NAME _____

Each one of these male singers, group or band has recorded a particular song with a female singer either as a duet or a song that featured a female singer. You are given the name of the male singer(s) and the initials of the well known song they did together and all you have to do is find the name of the female singer and the song. They are in a random order.

	MALE SINGER (or Group)	SONG INITALS	FEMALE SINGER	SONG
Ex.	Frank Sinatra	SS	Nancy Sinatra	Something Stupid
1.	Bill Medley	(IH)TTOML		
2.	John Travolta	YTOTIW		
3.	Marvin Gaye	TOS		
4.	Bryan Adams	WYG		
5.	Neil Diamond	YDBMF		
6.	Elton John	DGBMH		
7.	Serge Gainsbourg	JT..MNP (in French)		
8.	Robbie Williams	SS		
9.	Joe Cocker	UWWB		
10.	Nat King Cole	U		
11.	Shakin' Stevens	ARGW		
12.	The Bee Gees	I		
13.	Jason Donovan	EFY		
14.	Take That	RMF		
15.	Marvin Gaye	ITT		
16.	Kenny Rogers	IITS		
17.	George Michael	IKYWW(FM)		
18.	The Pet Shop Boys	WHIDTDT		
19.	Donnie Osmond	ILIAUTY		
20.	The Pogues	FONY		

32

33. HALF TIME QUIZ   TEAM NAME _____

	VENUE	SPORT
Ex.	Riverbank Arena	*Hockey*
1.	Box Hill	
2.	Earl's Court	
3.	Eton Dorney	
4.	ExCel, London	
5.	Greenwich Park	
6.	Hadleigh Farm, Essex	
7.	Hampton Court Palace	
8.	Horse Guards Parade	
9.	Hyde Park	
10.	Lee Valley Water Centre	
11.	Lord's Cricket Ground	
12.	North Greenwich Arena (O$_2$)	
13.	Olympic Park	
14.	Royal Artillery Barracks	
15.	St James's Park	
16.	Wembley Arena	
17.	Weymouth & Portland	
18.	Wimbledon	

LONDON OLYMPICS 2012

Match the sport's venue with the sport listed in the box

Archery
Badminton
Beach volleyball
Boxing
BMX Cycling
Canoe slalom
Equestrian
Football
Gymnastics (Artistic)
Hockey
Mountain Bike (cycling)
Road cycling
Road cycling time trial
Rowing
Sailing
Shooting
Tennis
Volleyball
10 km Swimming

THE OPENING CEREMONY

Who were the seven former Olympic medal winners who sponsored the young athletes who lit the Olympic torch ?

1.   2.
3.   4.
5.   6.
7.

7. During the opening ceremony which actor read an extract from Shakespeare's 'The Tempest' ?

8. Which band sung The Beatles 'Come Together' ?

9. Who opened the ceremony by ringing a bell ?

10. Which author read an extract from 'Peter Pan' ?

THE TORCH RELAY
1. How many (to the nearest 1000) torch bearers were there ?
        1000, 4000, 8000, or 10000

2. What metal was the torch mainly made from?

3. Where did the torch start its journey round the UK?

1. Where did Britain come in the final gold medal list?

2. Which band was the last to perform at the closing ceremony?

3. Which Royal represented the Queen at the closing ceremony?

Source 'london 2012.com'

34. HALF TIME QUIZ TEAM NAME _____

Except for the war years the Modern (Summer) Olympic Games have been held every 4 years since 1896. Can you fill in the cities on the table of Olympic cities since the war, plus the two yet to happen and then answer some questions about the Games.

Year	City
1948	
1952	
1956	
1960	
1964	
1968	
1972	
1976	
1980	
1984	
1988	
1992	
1996	
2000	
2004	
2008	
2012	
2016	
2020	

1. Only four cities have held the Olympic Games more than once, Athens, London and Los Angeles are three of them, what is the fourth one?
            ANSWER_____

2. The 1972 Olympic Games were marred by a dreadful event that nearly stopped the Games taking place. What happened?
  ANSWER_____

3. Sixty-two countries including the USA boycotted the Games in 1980. Why?

ANSWER_____

4. Two American athletes were expelled from the 1968 Games and stripped of their medals. Why did this happen? (It was nothing to do with drugs).

ANSWER_____

Some of the British gold medal winners for <u>athletic events</u> in 2012. Which event did they win?

1. Greg Rutherford	
2. Mo Farah (2 events)	
3. Jessica Ennis	
4. Alistair Brownlee	

Below are the names of some of gold medal winners in 2012 Can you write down the sport that each competitor did. You don't need the specific event, just the sport.

NAME	SPORT	NAME	SPORT
5. Luke Campbell		9. Ben Ainslie	
6. Laura Trott		10. Nicola Adams	
7. Peter Wilson		11. Ed McKeever	
8. Victoria Pendleton		12. Jade Jones	

35. HALF TIME QUIZ TEAM NAME _____

Can you indentify the town or city that the following English and Scottish league football clubs are either in or near.

	CLUB	TOWN or CITY
1.	Aston Villa	
2.	Everton	
3.	Heart of Midlothian	
4.	Hibernian	
5.	Partick Thistle	
6.	Port Vale	
7.	Queen of the South	
8.	Queens Park Rangers	
9.	St Johnstone	
10.	Tranmere Rovers	

Can you identify the sport associated with these venues.

11.	Bisley	
12.	Cowdray Park	
13.	Headingley	
14.	Hickstead	
15.	Ibrox	
16.	Lingfield Park	
17.	Murrayfield	
18.	Queen's Club	
19.	Rockingham	
20.	Turnberry	

With which sport do you associate these people.

21.	Jonah Barrington	
22.	Peter Ebdon	
23.	Kieran Fallon	
24.	Nancy Kerrigan	
25.	Jocky Wilson	

36. HALF TIME QUIZ TEAM NAME _____

All you have to do is fill in the gaps on the football ground table and the club nicknames. Then match the England football managers in the box at the bottom of the page with the years they were in charge.

<u>NOTE * - Caretaker manager on two occasions</u>

	CLUB	GROUND		YEARS	MANAGER
1.		Stadium of Light	1.	1963-74	
2.		Goodison Park	2.	1974	
3.	Fulham		3.	1974-77	
4.	Charlton Athletic		4.	1977-82	
5.		Villa Park	5.	1982-90	
6.	Leeds United		6.	1990-93	
7.		White Hart Lane	7.	1994-96	
8.		Anfield	8.	1996-99	
9.	Chelsea		9.	1999& 2000 *	
10.		Ibrox Park	10.	1999-00	

	CLUB	NICKNAME		YEARS	MANAGER
11.	Newcastle United		11.	2000-01	
12.	Birmingham City		12.	2001-06	
13.	Stoke City		13.	2006-07	
14.	Plymouth Argyle		14.	2008-11	
15.	Brighton & Hove Albion		15.	2012	
16.	Sheffield United		16.	2012-?	
17.	Liverpool				
18.	Norwich City				
19.	Manchester United				
20.	West Ham United				

Fabio Capello
Sven-Goran Eriksson
Ron Greenwood
Glen Hoddle
Roy Hodgson
Kevin Keegan
Steve McClaren
Joe Mercer
Stuart Pearce
Alf Ramsey
Don Revie
Bobby Robson
Graham Taylor
Peter Taylor
Terry Venables
Howard Wilkinson

Source 'Football Ground Guide & Colours of Football' & 'Englandfootballonline' Websites

37. HALF TIME QUIZ   TEAM NAME _____

Most breeds of dog are named after, either the place they come from, or a specific person who bred them originally. Can you name the breed of dog from the short description given. They are not in any specific order.

Ex. Terrier named after a northern British county   *Yorkshire Terrier*

1.	Very large rescue dog from Switzerland.	
2.	Long, short-legged German dog whose name means 'Badger hound'.	
3.	Small, white, long-haired terrier originally from Argyll in Scotland.	
4.	Small hound with floppy ears well known as Snoopy in 'Peanuts'.	
5.	Large brown short-haired dog from Zimbabwe with hair on its back running the opposite way from the rest of its hair.	
6.	Small poodle like dog with a French name meaning 'curly lap-dog'.	
7.	Medium sized muscular dog from a north midlands county.	
8.	Large powerful German dog often used as a guard dog.	
9.	Small dog that takes its name from a 17th Century English monarch.	
10.	Medium sized stocky dog with a 'squashed' muzzle from Germany	
11.	Intelligent, popular, small terrier named after a 19th Century parson.	
12.	Medium sized German dog with a wiry coat and distinct thick beard.	
13.	Fast, short-haired dog related to greyhounds.	
14.	Stocky short muzzled Chinese dog with a curly tail, usually black or fawn.	
15.	Strong, large, long-haired dog from Canada, known as a rescue dog.	
16.	Small long-haired terrier from a Scottish island.	
17.	Hound with a long silky coat from an Asian country that's often at war.	
18.	Long low dog with a bushy tail whose name means 'dwarf dog' in Welsh.	
19.	Chinese large stocky 'Lion dog'.	
20.	Medium to large sized German guard dog named after its breeder.	
21.	Small Chinese long-haired toy dog similar to a Pekingese	
22.	Medium sized 'Carriage dog' originally from Croatia.	
23.	Small terrier named after a mining town in Northumberland.	
24.	Strong, intelligent, popular working dog, used by the police.	
25.	Popular medium sized family dog that is named after part of Canada.	
26.	Medium, very stocky short muzzled dog strongly associated with England.	
27.	Large Russian dog that looks a bit like a long haired silky greyhound.	
28.	Tallest but not the heaviest breed of dog in the World.	
29.	Intelligent herding dog from Southern Scotland and Northern England.	
30.	Mexican 'Toy dog'.	
31.	Medium to large long-haired dog well known for advertising paint.	

38. HALF TIME QUIZ   TEAM NAME _____

What is the common name for these bones in the human body ?

1.	Patella	
2.	Phananges	
3.	Mandible	
4.	Femur	
5.	Clavicle	
6.	Sternum	
7.	Tibia	
8.	Scapula	

Where are these glands to be found in the human body ?

9.	Thyroid Gland	
10.	Islets of Langerhans	
11.	Adrenal Glands	
12.	Pituitary Gland	
13.	Gall Bladder	
14.	Sublingual Gland	

In which organs can these 'things' be found ?

15.	Tricuspid valve	
16.	Vitreous humour	
17.	Occipital lobe	
18.	Alveoli	
19.	Pyloric sphincter	
20.	Olfactory Cell	
21.	Ossicles	
22.	Medulla and Cortex	

Where are these muscles in the body ?

23.	Deltoid	
24.	Soleus	
25.	Gluteus Maximus	
26.	Pectoral	
27.	Triceps	
28.	Masseter	
29.	Quadriceps	
30.	Trapezius	

Source - Medical encyclopedia, published by Guild Publishing

39. HALF TIME QUIZ   TEAM NAME _____

Below are twenty questions about couples, some are actual people and some are fictitious. Most are romantically linked in some way through songs, films, TV, celebrity gossip or history, all you have to do is answer the questions.

Ex.	Ashley and Cheryl married in 2006. What was her surname before her marriage?	*Tweedy*
1.	Where did Jack and Rose meet?	
2.	While Desmond had a barrow in the local market, what was Molly?	
3.	What did David and Elizabeth do for Diana in 1981?	
4.	What genre of music were Cleo and Johnny involved in?	
5.	How did Tommy and Gina live according to the 1987 song title?	
6.	What kind of life did Tom and Barbara choose to live?	
7.	How did Henry punish Ann's adultery?	
8.	How did Katy meet Peter (now separated!)?	
9.	Where, in London, did Terry meet Julie every Friday night?	
10.	Harvard graduates, Oliver and Jennifer's, romance ended tragically. What happened?	
11.	Tony and Maria met on the back streets of New York in which film?	
12.	Who sang about Bonnie and Clyde and their violent end in 1967?	
13.	After Adam and Eve 'misbehaved' in Eden, what specific curse did God bestow on Eve?	
14.	William and Mary were 'in charge' in the 1600s. Where had William come from originally?	
15.	After Sam died, which actress played his 'medium' link that allowed him to communicate with Molly?	
16.	Jim's happy marriage to Dot was threatened by his health problems. What happened to him?	
17.	Although not romantically linked, Jayne and Chris are frequently seen very close together. Why?	
18.	What did Tommy want to tell Laura after his crash before he died?	
19.	Sophie and Sky are due to marry, but she is obsessed with finding her father, in which film?	
20.	Basil and Sybil had a stormy relationship running their hotel in which town?	

40. HALF TIME QUIZ   TEAM NAME _____

All the answers begin with the letter Q. To make things a little easier I have given you the second letter as well, (in most of them) !

Ex.	A district of New York.	*Queens*
1.	Small members of the partridge family of birds.	qu
2.	A source of radiation outside our galaxy.	qu
3.	Boggy ground.	qu
4.	An extinct member of the zebra family.	qu
5.	Westlife Number 1 in 2001	Qu
6.	A place at the south end of the Fourth Road Bridge.	Qu
7.	A square dance for four couples	qu
8.	The number of times a quantity is contained in another.	qu
9.	A hard silicon rock mineral	qu
10.	A 1979 rock musical featuring music from 'The Who'	Qu
11.	A measure of paper.	qu
12.	1952 film starring John Wayne about a boxer.	The Qu
13.	Middle eastern state.	Q
14.	Old fashioned expression meaning 'to be in debt'.	To be in qu
15.	Capital of Ecuador	Qu
16.	Somerset Hills	The Qu
17.	An adventure or expedition for a specific purpose	qu
18.	Sc-fi TV serial created in the 50s and revived in 1979	Qu
19.	Blyton's 'Famous Five' uncle to Julian, Dick and Ann.	Qu
20.	Singer (female, surname) had a 1973 hit with initials CTC	Qu
21.	Half a crotchet.	qu
22.	The 'Religious Society of Friends'.	Qu
23.	American actor (Surname) once married to Meg Ryan.	Qu
24.	Writing fluid first sold in 1931	Qu
25.	First World War submarine decoy vessels.	Q
26.	TV shopping channel	Q
27.	American TV series set in LA about a Medical Examiner	Qu

41. HALF TIME QUIZ TEAM NAME _____

All the answers begin with the letter U.

Ex.	A range of mountains in Russia	*Urals*
1.	Ayer's Rock	U
2.	One of the Crosby & Hope 'Road' films	Road to U
3.	Take possession by force or to assume authority	u
4.	Lake District lake.	U
5.	Of a bear	u
6.	1987 film set in Chicago, in the prohibition era.	The U
7.	"Unsightly" Essex village!	U
8.	A long loose overcoat.	u
9.	Region of central Italy	U
10.	4 times No. 1 song, first recorded by Jimmy Young	U
11.	Dead creature found in the Forbidden Forest in the first Harry Potter book.	u
12.	Norwegian actress (surname), starred in 'A Bridge Too Far'	U
13.	Town associated with Stan Laurel	U
14.	Country south of Kazakhstan.	U
15.	Middle Eastern country on the Persian Gulf	U
16.	1992 Western starring Clint Eastwood	U
17.	'Aunt Sally' actress (Christian name).	U
18.	Roman TV sit com of the 70s	U
19.	Small port in NW Scotland	U
20.	Dylan Thomas play set in a Welsh seaside town.	U
21.	2007 Rihanna song that made No. 1	U
22.	Famous Flanagan & Allen wartime song	U
23.	Song that starts "When the sun shines on the mountains, and the night is on the run"	U
24.	Trade name of some sticky stuff!	U
25.	The darker part of a shadow	u
26.	Southern German city	U

42. HALF TIME QUIZ TEAM NAME_____

All the following answers end with the letters **ic** You just have to find the answers from the clues. The answers are 3, 4, 5 or 6 letters long. For Example:-

Poisonous   *Toxic*

1.	Stylishly fashionable	
2.	Abdominal pain	
3.	Relating to iron	
4.	Endure hardship without complaining	
5.	Muscle spasm of the face	
6.	Anything that causes vomiting	
7.	Stationary	
8.	Scandinavian	
9.	Dice shaped	
10.	Savoury jelly	
11.	Scottish language	
12.	Relating to the universe	
13.	Children's paper !	
14.	Relating to sexual matters	
15.	Medieval architectural style particularly of churches	
16.	Relating to a town's administration	
17.	Relating to a circle	
18.	Rural charm	
19.	Relating to an infected wound	
20.	Classical architectural style with fluted columns	
21.	Historical artefact	
22.	Harmonised sounds produced to provide pleasure	
23.	French	
24.	Old London Shakespearian theatre	
25.	Like vinegar	

43. HALF TIME QUIZ   TEAM NAME _____

The English language has adopted a large number of words from other languages. Listed below are some words that originated from other languages. All you have to do is match the language of origin, to the word in the list. In the box there is a selection of languages to choose from, but beware, not every one can be matched to a word, and some may be needed more than once.

Ex.	telephone	*Greek*
1.	puffin	
2.	zero	
3.	bungalow	
4.	penguin	
5.	yacht	
6.	tsunami	
7.	camouflage	
8.	patio	
9.	sauna	
10.	blarney	
11.	kidnap	
12.	debris	
13.	slalom	
14.	guitar	
15.	impala	
16.	calendar	
17.	autumn	
18.	tycoon	
19.	lychee	
20.	corgi	
21.	dahlia	
22.	dungarees	
23.	amen	
24.	tornado	
25.	dinghy	

LATIN HINDI JAPANESE DUTCH DANISH FRENCH EGYPTIAN ARABIC BENGALI WELSH ZULU THAI CANTONESE KOREAN SPANISH POLISH NORSE SWEDISH NORWEGIAN CORNISH HEBREW GAELIC FINNISH ITALIAN

Source   KryssTal.com Website

HALF TIME QUIZ   TEAM NAME_____

The following well known books titles have "lost their vowels and 'y's". Can you find them and work out the titles . They are not in any particular order.

EXAMPLE Lttl Wmn	*Little Women*
1. Lrn Dn	
2. Vnt Fr	
3. tl f tw cts	
4. Th D Vnc Cd	
5. nml Frm	
6. Ivnh	
7. Wthrng Hghts	
8. Th Stnc Vrss	
9. Brghtn Rck	
10. Ic n Wndrlnd	
11. Th cll f th wld	
12. mm	
13. Th d f th trffds	
14. Brn Fr	
15. Lrd Jm	
16. Blck Bt	
17. Brchstr Twrs	
18. Mb Dck	
19. Wtrshp Dwn	
20. Lck Jm	
21. ncl Tm's Cbn	
22. Trsr Islnd	
23. T kll mckng brd	
24. Ld Chttrl's lvr	
25. Th thrt-nn stps	
26. Fft shds f gr	

45. HALF TIME QUIZ TEAM NAME _____

All you have to do is identify the country to which each National Flag belongs. However there's no colour to help so you have to rely only on the design to find the right answer.

Example

Israel

1
2
3
4
5
6
7
8
9
10
11
12
13
14
15
16
17
18
19
20
21
22

1.
2.
3.
4.
5.
6.
7.
8.
9.
10
11
12
13
14
15
16
17
18
19
20
21
22

46. HALF TIME QUIZ TEAM NAME_____

The London Underground is the oldest and most extensive Underground network in the world. On the left are 13 line colours used on the standard underground map, all you have to do is identify the lines they indicate. Below that are a list of outer terminus stations, you also have to indicate the lines you would have to take to reach them.

	COLOUR	LINE
1.	Blue	
2.	Pale Blue	
3.	Very Pale Blue	
4.	Red	
5.	Deep Pink	
6.	Pale Pink	
7.	Orange	
8.	Yellow	
9.	Brown	
10.	Green	
11.	Deep Blue-Green	
12.	Grey	
13.	Black	

	TERMINUS	LINE
1.	Heathrow Airport	
2.	Amersham	
3.	Stanmore	
4.	Edgware	
5.	Epping	
6.	Upminster	
7.	Lewisham	
8.	New Cross	
9.	Brixton	
10.	Morden	
11.	Wimbledon	
12.	Richmond	

Which underground lines pass through the following London stations. The number in brackets is the number of lines.

	STATION	LINES
1.	Victoria (3)	
2.	Waterloo (4)	
3.	Euston (2)	
4.	Liverpool Street (4)	

5. Which line was the first to open with steam trains in 1863?

_____

6. Which line opened on 9-1-1968?

_____

7. Before 1977 the Jubilee line was known by another name. What was it?

_____

8. What was Henry Beck's contribution to the London Underground system in 1933?

47. HALF TIME QUIZ TEAM NAME _____

Starting with Kent, this is a 'round Britain quiz' of natural coastal features.
There is a clue to the feature and where it is, all you have to do is name it.

EXAMPLE	Island off the north coast of Kent	*Isle of Sheppey*

1.	Flat, open area, in south Kent, with a lighthouse at its tip.	
2.	Cliff at the eastern end of the South Downs	
3.	Headland in W. Sussex near where Sir Patrick Moore lived.	
4.	Chalk stacks and rocks off the western tip of the IOW.	
5.	Large island in Poole Harbour.	
6.	Small circular cove on the Dorset coast.	
7.	The most southerly point on the British mainland.	
8.	An island connected by a causeway to Marazion.	
9.	The most westerly point of the British mainland	
10.	Bird sanctuary island about 25 miles west of Ilfracombe.	
11.	South Wales peninsular near Swansea.	
12.	Large bay stretching from Pembrokeshire to Gwynedd.	
13.	Island off the NW coast of Wales.	
14.	A peninsular between the Rivers Dee and Mersey.	
15.	Long narrow island off Barrow in Furness.	
16.	Island about half way between Cumbria and Ireland.	
17.	Scottish headland immortalised by 'Wings'.	
18.	Island well known for its wool and chunky sweaters!	
19.	The largest island of the Outer Hebrides.	
20.	The most northerly group of islands off Scotland.	
21.	Island connected by a causeway to the Northumbria coast .	
22.	Group of islands off Northumbria known for their seabirds.	
23.	Headland in Yorkshire close to Bridlington.	
24.	Large river estuary separating Yorkshire from Lincolnshire.	
25.	Sea area between Lincolnshire and Norfolk.	
26.	Essex headland with the seaside village of Walton on it.	
27.	Island off the south coast of Essex in the Thames Estuary	

48. HALF TIME QUIZ   TEAM NAME _____

This is all about places in Britain. All you have to do is write down the answers!!

Ex	What is the most northerly town in England?	*Berwick on Tweed*
1.	What is the closest town to Ben Nevis?	
2.	Which Scottish Island has a place called Uig on it?	
3.	Which city has a medieval street called 'The Shambles'?	
4.	In which town can you find the longest pleasure pier in the World?	
5.	Which northern town has a 'Transporter Bridge'?	
6.	In which Welsh town can you find 'Britain's smallest house'?	
7.	What is said to be 'The earliest recorded town in England'?	
8.	On which island can you find the place with the longest name?	
9.	In which city can you find 'The Cavern' night club?	
10.	In which town was Stan Laurel born?	
11.	In which city is 'The Royal Mile'?	
12.	In which town is the most easterly point in Britain?	
13.	In which town was 'Boots' (the chemist) first established?	
14.	On which Scottish island is 'Fingal's Cave'?	
15.	Which town is the site of the worst air disaster in Britain?	
16.	In which city is 'The Bodleian Library'?	
17.	In which town is 'The Metro Centre' shopping complex?	
18.	In which city is 'The Coleman's mustard shop'?	
19.	Which town is Robert Burns most associated with?	
20.	In which city is 'The Millennium Stadium'?	
21.	From which city did Francis Chichester sail in 1966?	
22.	Which city is known as 'The Granite City?	
23.	On which island did Queen Victoria die in 1901?	
24.	In which city can you find 'The Royal Crescent'?	
25.	In which city is the cathedral featured on the old £20 note?	
26.	In which city's cathedral is the medieval 'Mappa Mundi'?	
27.	In which town was Margaret Thatcher born?	
28.	In which city is the Tudor shopping mall called 'The Rows'?	

49. HALF TIME QUIZ   TEAM NAME _____

This is all about places in Britain. All you have to do is write down the answers!!

Ex	Which city's cathedral was destroyed on the 14th Nov. 1940?	*Coventry*
1.	Which Oxfordshire town is famous for making blankets?	
2.	In which city's cathedral is the tomb of 'The Black Prince' ?	
3.	Which city has a statue of King Alfred on its main street?	
4.	Of which island group are Unst, Yell and Fetler part of?	
5.	In which town was Oliver Cromwell born in 1599?	
6.	In which city can you find 'Temple Meads Station'?	
7.	Which town is at the north east end of Loch Ness?	
8.	What is 'Holy Island' also known as?	
9.	Which Essex new town is just north of Epping?	
10.	On which island was the first scout camp set up?	
11.	Which town is on the northern side of the Tay Bridge?	
12.	Which Cornish village was nearly destroyed by a flood in 2004	
13.	From which town does the famous 'mint cake' come from?	
14.	In which city did the 'Wests' murder most of their victims?	
15.	On which Island is the town of Douglas?	
16.	Which Yorkshire town has a strong association with whaling?	
17.	Which town is on the west side of Portmouth Harbour?	
18.	Which city is associated with the manufacture of cutlery?	
19.	In which city was the 'Harland and Wolff' shipyard?	
20.	To which Welsh town did 'Fiddler's Dram' have a day trip to?	
21.	In which town can you find 'The Pleasure Beach Theme Park'?	
22.	In which city can you find the towns of Fenton & Longton?	
23.	Which town is at the eastern end of Hadrian's Wall?	
24.	In which city were Rowntree's and Terry's chocolates made?	
25.	In which village graveyard is William Wordsworth buried?	
26.	Which Welsh town is near Great Ormes Head?	
27.	Which city has the cathedral with the tallest spire?	
28.	From which town did Gilbert & Sullivan's pirates come from?	

50. HALF TIME QUIZ   TEAM NAME _____

This is all about places in Britain. All you have to do is write down the answers!!

Ex	With which city is 'Cadbury's Chocolate' most associated with ?	*Birmingham*
1.	Which 'bird sanctuary' island is 12 miles north of Devon?	
2.	In which county can you find Kempton Park race course	
3.	Where, in Scotland, did the Campbells massacre the McDonalds in 1692?	
4.	Over which river did the railway bridge collapse in 1879?	
5.	In the Hardy novel, which Dorset town represents Casterbridge ?	
6.	In which city did 'Burke and Hare' murder for profit in 1827?	
7.	In which Essex town were the first public broadcasts made in 1922?	
8.	In which Northern Irish county is the 'Giant's Causeway ?	
9.	Which Welsh city is the smallest by population in the UK ?	
10.	In which UK country was Princess Margaret born in 1930?	
11.	Of which city is Toxteth, Huyton and Wavertree part of?	
12.	What is the nearest Scottish town to John O'Groats?	
13.	In which city is the 'Sally Lunn Bakery'	
14.	In which National Park can you find Ringwood and Brockenhurst?	
15.	Which northern town did super-sized MP Cyril Smith represent?	
16.	In which part of London was 'Only Fools & Horses' set?	
17.	In which part of the UK will you find Strabane & Coleraine ?	
18.	The 'New Vaudeville Band' sang about which city's cathedral?	
19.	In which Cornish town will you find 'Rick Stein's' restaurant?	
20.	As well as Workington, which other Cumbrian town was flooded in Nov. 2009.	
21.	In which county is Donington Park motor racing circuit?	
22.	From which Kent town did Mick Jagger come ?	
23.	Which motor manufacturer is closely linked with Derby ?	
24.	Which writer lived in Laugharne in Wales?	
25.	In which county is the site of the first iron bridge ever built in 1779?	
26.	To which seaside resort did 'Chas & Dave' go in 1982?	
27.	In which city is Headingley cricket ground ?	
28.	Which prison can be found near Princetown in Devon?	

51. HALF TIME QUIZ TEAM NAME _____

The clues below should lead you to a **British** TOWN/CITY, RIVER or COUNTY that has only **4 letters** in its name. To give you a little extra help the answers are in alphabetical order. A few first letters are included on the more difficult ones.

Ex.	South-eastern English county.	*Kent*
1.	Yorkshire river that passes through the county town.	_ _ _ _
2.	Shakespeare's home town's river !	_ _ _ _
3.	West country Roman town with a hot spring.	_ _ _ _
4.	North Cornish holiday resort.	_ _ _ _
5.	Northern town between Rochdale and Bolton.	B _ _ _
6.	Kentish coastal town with a castle,	_ _ _ _
7.	Small Norfolk market town.	D _ _ _
8.	Northern Irish county.	_ _ _ _
9.	Small Berkshire town with top school.	_ _ _ _
10.	Scottish county between the Tay and the Forth.	_ _ _ _
11.	Partner to Brighton.	_ _ _ _
12.	City on the north side of the Humber estuary.	_ _ _ _
13.	Small market town near Stoke-on Trent in Staffordshire.	L _ _ _
14.	Cornish port and tourist town on the south coast.	_ _ _ _
15.	Town on Romney Marsh in Kent with a small airport nearby.	L _ _ _
16.	Welsh town in Flintshire	M _ _ _
17.	Major river in Eastern England that flows into The Wash	_ _ _ _
18.	Loch with a myth attached !	_ _ _ _
19.	West coast Scottish fishing port and tourist centre.	_ _ _ _
20.	Small town on the IOM.	P _ _ _
21.	Seaside resort on the north Welsh coast.	_ _ _ _
22.	IOW seaside resort.	_ _ _ _
23.	Town within Greater Manchester, whose name suggests a bargain !	S _ _ _
24.	District of London whose name was derived from a hunting cry.	_ _ _ _
25.	Second longest river in Scotland.	S _ _ _
26.	River that forms the border between Durham and Yorkshire.	_ _ _ _
27.	Northern river that flows into the North Sea, once famous for shipbuilding.	_ _ _ _
28.	Hertfordshire town famous for its great bed mentioned in 'Twelfth Night'.	_ _ _ _
29.	Almost the most northern mainland Scottish town.	_ _ _ _
30.	Northern city with walls and a very big minster.	_ _ _ _

52. HALF TIME QUIZ   TEAM NAME_____

There are 30 places in England listed below but in each the 1st, 3rd, 5th and so on letters are missing. You have to identify the place. It maybe a tourist attraction, region, transport or sports venue. The word THE is <u>not</u> included in any of them.

EX.	-O-E- C-S-L-	DOVER CASTLE
1.	-I-T-E- R-C-C-U-S-	
2.	-O-F-L- B-O-D-	
3.	-A-D- E-D	
4.	-H-T-Y -B-E-	
5.	-H-P-N-D- Z-O	
6.	-U-B-R -R-D-E	
7.	-S-O-N- H-U-E	
8.	-O-E- O- L-N-O-	
9.	-L- T-A-F-R- C-I-K-T -R-U-D	
10.	-A-T-R-U-Y -A-H-D-A-	
11.	-A-E D-S-R-C-	
12.	-O-C-M-E -A-	
13.	-M- V-C-O-Y	
14.	-T-N-H-N-E	
15.	-O-A- L-V-R -U-L-I-G	
16.	-H-R-O-D F-R-S-	
17.	-A-T-O-R	
18.	-A-I-N-L -O-O- M-S-U-	
19.	-E- F-R-S-	
20.	-I-D-O- C-S-L-	
21.	-R-G-T-N -A-I-I-N	
22.	-I-A- -I-R	
23.	-E-B-E- S-A-I-M	
24.	-D-N -R-J-C-	
25.	-A-C-I-F- C-M-R-	
26.	-A-C-E-T-R -I-P-R-	
27.	-I-V-R-T-N-	
28.	-L-N-E-M -A-A-E	
29.	-O-E-T-Y C-T-E-R-L	
30.	-A-R-A-'S -A-L	

53. HALF TIME QUIZ TEAM NAME _____

All the answers to the clues or questions fit a pattern. After you have done a few of the easy ones and discovered the pattern the harder ones should become easier. Two are impossible, you'll see why when you've found the pattern

1.	Middle-eastern market.	
2.	Very popular word game invented in 1938 in America.	
3.	Surname of the producer of most of the Bond movies.	
4.	Violinist, crook or type of crab.	
5.	Branded item for blowing your nose on.	
6.	"I'll be back in a ...."	
7.	A Jim Henson muppet or animated TV series, ... Rock !	
8.	Essential item for an angler.	
9.	The place not to have been when Vesuvius erupted in 79 AD.	
10.	The pilgrimage to Mecca that all Muslims must take.	
11.	A person who goes on a long journey by foot in South Africa.	
12.	The band who created the song 'Human' in 2008.	
13.	Shark resembling a carpenter's tool.	
14.	Vegetable with an aniseed taste.	
15.	First word of Lulu's Eurovision song of 1969.	
16.	African 'river-horse'.	
17.	IMPOSSIBLE	############
18.	Christian name of Shirley MacLaine's brother.	
19.	Serpent sound.	
20.	The animal featured in 'Ring of Bright Water'.	
21.	Space with literally nothing in it.	
22.	A man employed to dig roads / railways / tunnels etc.	
23.	American Indian ceremony of dancing and feasting.	
24.	The name of an American oil and petrol company.	
25.	IMPOSSIBLE	############
26.	Tommy Roe 1969 song, also recorded by comedian Vic Reeves.	

54. HALF TIME QUIZ   TEAM NAME _____

The answers to each of these questions is a number. You have a choice of 5 possible answers and all you have to do is ring the correct one.   None of them are "years". Example:-

The men who marched with the Duke   500   1000   5000   (10,000)   20,000

#	Question	Choices
1.	The number of men who have walked on the moon	10 12 14 16 18
2.	The number of cards in a Tarot pack.	45 52 64 78 86
3.	The number of miles from Land's End to John O'Groats	765 815 854 876 966
4.	To the nearest mph, the speed 20 knots converts to	18 20 23 25 28
5.	The height of a horse of 18 hands in feet	5 5.5 6 6.5 7 7.5
6.	The number of feet in 100 fathoms.	400 500 600 800 1000
7.	The number of years Halley's Comet takes to revisit Earth	56 66 76 86 96
8.	The minimum number of points needed to win a set in tennis.	18 24 30 36 42
9.	The motorway number that links Manchester with Leeds	6 18 55 57 62
10.	The length of Queen Victoria's reign, (in years)	55 60 63 67 69
11.	The number of yds. from the penalty spot to the goal line (football).	10 12 15 18 20
12.	The number represented by MDCLIV in Roman numerals	946 1046 1454 1556 1654
13.	The number of players in a basketball team	5 6 7 8 9
14.	The size of a Scottish jury	10 12 14 15 18
15.	The number of stars in Orion's belt.	3 5 6 7 8
16.	The number of countries that border Germany	5 6 7 8 9
17.	The average of the sum of the first 20 consecutive numbers	9.5 10 10.25 10.5 10.75
18.	The number of keys on a standard piano	64 72 80 88 96
19.	You've read 30% of a book of 370 pages. How many pages?	97 101 111 117 121
20.	The value of x in this equation — $3(x - 2) = 18$	-8 -7 7 8 10
21.	The length of a marathon (nearest mile).	22 24 25 26 27
22.	The number of letters in the French alphabet	22 24 25 26 27
23.	The length of one side of a square with a perimeter of 12 metres	3 4 24 48 144
24.	4 cubed	12 16 32 64 96
25.	The number of faces on a triangular prism	3 5 8 10 12
26.	The number of sides on an old 3d piece.	8 9 10 11 12
27.	The number of countries in South America	12 13 14 15 16
28.	The number of shillings 5 guineas was worth	85 90 95 100 105
29.	The number of human gifts sent on the twelfth day of Christmas	50 55 60 125 364
30.	The number of hoops on a croquet court	10 12 16 18 20
31.	The percentage of the Earth's surface covered by water.	50 60 65 70 75

55. HALF TIME QUIZ TEAM NAME _____

How well do you know South America? All you have to do is match the names of the countries in South and Central America with the numbers on the map.

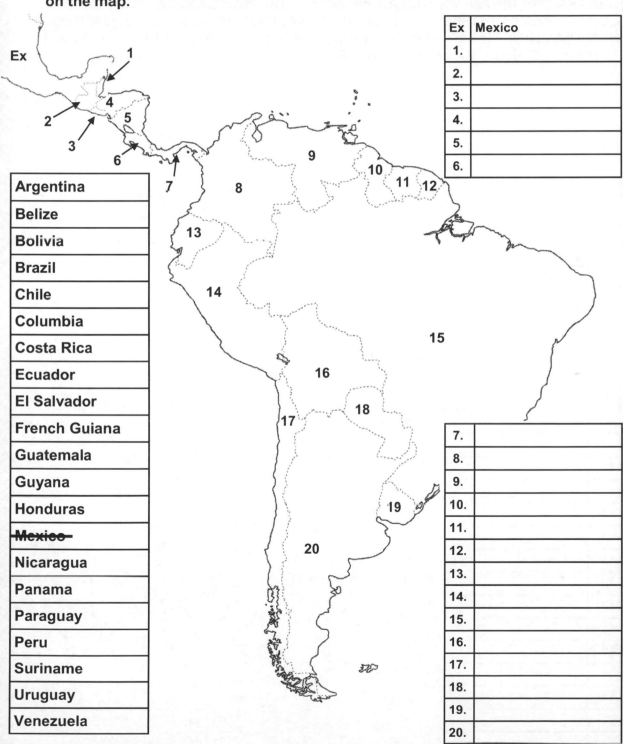

Ex	Mexico
1.	
2.	
3.	
4.	
5.	
6.	

Argentina

Belize

Bolivia

Brazil

Chile

Columbia

Costa Rica

Ecuador

El Salvador

French Guiana

Guatemala

Guyana

Honduras

~~**Mexico**~~

Nicaragua

Panama

Paraguay

Peru

Suriname

Uruguay

Venezuela

7.	
8.	
9.	
10.	
11.	
12.	
13.	
14.	
15.	
16.	
17.	
18.	
19.	
20.	

56. HALF TIME QUIZ TEAM NAME _____

All you have to do is match the names of the countries in Africa with the numbers on the map. The names are:- ALGERIA, ANGOLA, BOTSWANA, CAMEROON, CENTRAL AFRICAN REPUBLIC, ~~EGYPT,~~ ETHIOPIA, GAMBIA, GHANA, IVORY COAST, KENYA, LIBERIA, LIBYA, MADAGASCAR, MOROCCO, MOZAMBIQUE, NAMIBIA, NIGERIA, SOMALIA, SIERRA LEONE, SOUTH AFRICA, TANZANIA, TUNISIA, UGANDA, ZAMBIA, ZIMBABWE

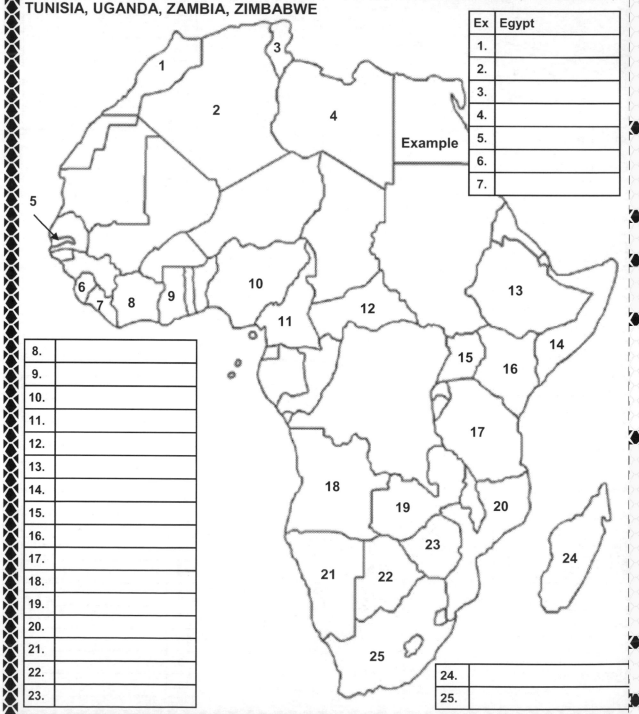

Ex	Egypt
1.	
2.	
3.	
4.	
5.	
6.	
7.	

8.	
9.	
10.	
11.	
12.	
13.	
14.	
15.	
16.	
17.	
18.	
19.	
20.	
21.	
22.	
23.	

24.	
25.	

57. HALF TIME QUIZ TEAM NAME _____

This is the Great Lakes area of Canada and the USA. Can you name the five lakes marked L1 to L5, the cities marked A to E and the American states marked 1 to 5. Choose your answers from the box at the bottom.

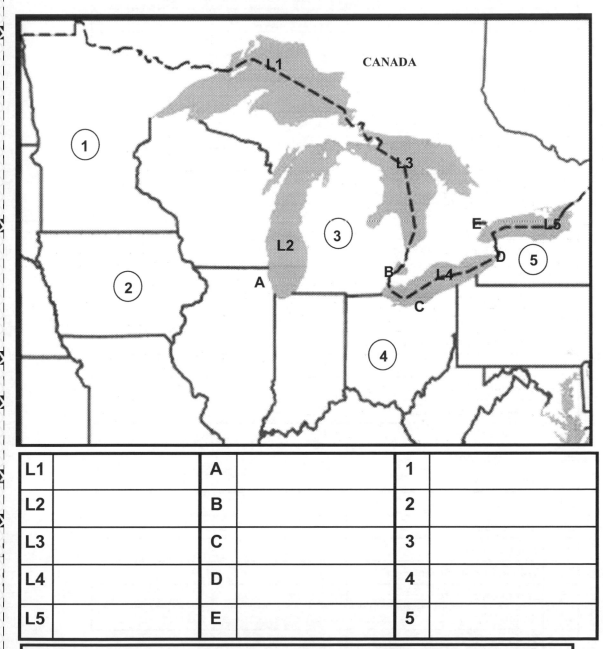

L1		A		1	
L2		B		2	
L3		C		3	
L4		D		4	
L5		E		5	

Buffalo, Chicago, Cleveland, Detroit, Erie, Huron, Iowa, Michigan (Lake), Michigan (State), Minnesota, New York, Ohio, Ontario, Superior, Toronto

58. HALF TIME QUIZ   TEAM NAME _____

There are 25 inventers or discoverers listed below. Some are only credited with inventing the "thing" when, in fact others may have done much of the work. You need to find what they invented or discovered. They are not in any particular order.

	NAME	INVENTION or DISCOVERY
1.	Charles Babbage	
2.	Joseph Swan	
3.	Percy Shaw	
4.	Alfred Nobel	
5.	George Eastman	
6.	Wilhelm Rontgen	
7.	James Dyson	
8.	Humphrey Davey	
9.	Johann Gutenberg	
10.	Sir Henry Cole	
11.	Robert Oppenheimer	
12.	Adolphe Sax	
13.	Igor Sikorsky	
14.	Jacques Cousteau	
15.	Alexander Graham Bell	
16.	Tim Berners-Lee	
17.	Rowland Hill	
18.	Christopher Cockerell	
19.	Trevor Bayliss	
20.	Emile Berliner	
21.	Richard Gatling	
22.	Guglielmo Marconi	
23.	Laszlo Biro	
24.	James Dewer	
25.	Willian Friese-Greene	
26.	John Logie Baird	
27.	Samuel Colt	
28.	Thomas Edison	
29.	Steve Jobs	
30.	Joseph & Jacques Mongolfier	
31.	Arthur Wynne	
32.	Richard Trevithick	

59. HALF TIME QUIZ   TEAM NAME_____

The following people 'went before their time', ! They all died before they should have from various different causes in the years given. All you have to do is write down how they died. It is not good enough just to write 'accident', 'executed' or 'died from a disease', more detail must be given. For example:-

Diana, Princess of Wales   1997   *Car accident in Paris*

1.	William II	1100	
2.	Edward II	1327	
3.	Catherine Howard	1542	
4.	Thomas Cranmer	1556	
5.	Spencer Perceval	1812	
6.	Prince Albert	1861	
7.	T E Lawrence	1935	
8.	Glenn Miller	1944	
9.	Joseph Goebbles	1945	
10.	Marylyn Monroe	1962	
11.	Jim Reeves	1964	
12.	Jayne Mansfield	1967	
13.	Tony Hancock	1968	
14.	Graham Hill	1975	
15.	Natalie Wood	1981	
16.	Marvin Gaye	1984	
17.	Laura Ashley	1985	
18.	Roy Kinnear	1988	
19.	Freddie Mercury	1991	
20.	Ayrton Senna	1994	
21.	Eva Cassidy	1996	
22.	Sonny Bono	1998	
23.	Jill Dando	1999	
24.	Donald Dewar MP	2000	
25.	Kirsty McCall	2000	
26.	Natasha Richardson	2009	
27.	Amy Winehouse	2011	

60. HALF TIME QUIZ   TEAM NAME _____

Thirteen Prime Ministers have served Britain since the War. Can you match the constituency they represented with their names? Underneath are the names of twelve well known MPs of past and present, can you do the same for them?

	POST WAR PRIME MINISTERS	CONSTITUENCY
1.	Clement Atlee	
2.	Winston Churchill	
3.	Anthony Eden	
4.	Harold Macmillan	
5.	Sir Alec Douglas Home	
6	Harold Wilson	
7	Edward Heath	
8	James Callaghan	
9	Margaret Thatcher	
10.	John Major	
11.	Tony Blair	
12.	Gordon Brown	
13.	David Cameron	

P.M. CONSTITUENCIES

Huntindon
Cardiff SE
Witney
Kinross & West
    Perthshire
Huyton
Sedgefield
Bexley
Walthamstow West
Finchley
Kirkcaldy &
    Cowdenbeath
Woodford
Warwick &
    Leamington
Bromley

	Well Known MPs	CONSTITUENCY
1.	Paddy Ashdown	
2.	Betty Boothroyd	
3.	Nick Clegg	
4.	Sebastian Coe	
5.	Dennis Healey	
6	Boris Johnson	
7	Charles Kennedy	
8	Ed Miliband	
9	Cyril Smith	
10.	Anthony Wedgewood Benn	
11.	Ann Widdecombe	
12.	Shirley Williams	

OTHER CONSTITUENCIES

Leeds East
Sheffield Hallam
Chesterfield
Maidstone & The
    Weald
Yeovil
Doncaster North
Crosby
West Bromwich
Ross, Skye &
    Lochaber
Falmouth &
    Camborne
Henley
Rochdale

61. HALF TIME QUIZ TEAM NAME _____

All the days on the left hand table are fixed dates in the UK Calendar, (the Equinoxes and Solstices can vary by a day or so). All you have to do is match the dates to the days. The other table has some "I remember where I was" dates to find, (the year of some events is not needed). There are some extra questions as well at the bottom.

	DAY	DATE
Ex.	Christmas Day	*25th December*
1.	All Fool's Day	
2.	All Saints Day	
3.	All Souls Day	
4.	Armistice Day	
5.	Autumnal Equinox	
6.	Battle of Britain Day	
7.	Burns Night	
8.	Coronation Day (QE II)	
9.	Epiphany	
10.	Guy Fawkes' Night	
11.	Halloween	
12.	Hogmanay	
13.	May Day	
14.	Midsummer's Day	
15.	St Andrew's Day	
16.	St David's Day	
17.	St George's Day	
18.	St Patrick's Day	
19.	St Stephen's Day	
20.	St Swithun's Day	
21.	St Valentine's Day	
22.	Summer Solstice	
23.	The Queen's Birthday	
24.	Vernal Equinox	
25.	Winter Solstice	

	OTHER DAYS	DATE
1.	American Independence Day	
2.	Destruction of the World Trade Centre	
3.	Assassination of President Kennedy	
4.	The Death of Diana Princess of Wales	
5.	The Death of John Lennon	
6.	The Bombs in London in 2005	

7. On which day of the week are General Elections held in;-

a) The UK_____

b) The USA_____

8. What is the name of the day that precedes the first day of Lent?

_____

9. In the Christian calendar what is the 7th Sunday after Easter known as?

62. HALF TIME QUIZ   TEAM NAME _____

On the left is a list of makes and models of cars that have been used in well known films & TV programs. On the right are the programs and films, match one to the other. The given year refers to that of the approximate manufacture of the car used in the production.

Ex.	Reliant Regal (1969)	*Only Fools & Horses*
1.	Aston Martin DB5 (1963)	
2.	Audi Quattro (1980)	
3.	Austin 1100 (1967)	
4.	BMC Mini 1000 (1970)	
5.	Cadillac Miller-Meteor Ambulance (1959)	
6.	Dodge Charger R/T (1969)	
7.	Delorean DMC-12 (1981)	
8.	Ferrari Daytona Spyder (1972)	
9.	Ford Anglia 105E (1959)	
10.	Ford Capri Mk III (1978)	
11.	Ford Cortina Mk III (1974)	
12.	Ford Granada Mk II (1977)	
13.	Ford Gran Torino (1974)	
14.	Ford Model T (1927)	
15.	Ford Zephyr Mk II (1962)	
16.	Jaguar E-Type (1970)	
17.	Jaguar Mk II (1960)	
18.	Lotus Esprit S1 (1977)	
19.	Mini Cooper S (1967)	
20.	Morris Minor 1000 (1967)	
21.	Peugeot 403 (1959)	
22.	Pontiac Trans-Am (1982)	
23.	Range Rover (1970)	
24.	Rolls Royce Landaulet (1929)	
25.	Rover 200 SD3 (1987)	
26.	Triumph Roadster 1800 (1947)	
27.	Volkswagen Beetle (1963)	
28.	Volvo P1800 (1962)	

FILMS & TV PROGRAMMES

Ashes to Ashes
Austin Powers Films
Back to the Future Films
Bergerac
Columbo
Dukes of Hazzard
Fawlty Towers
Ghostbusters
Goldfinger
Harry Potter & the Chamber
  of Secrets
Herbie Rides Again
Keeping Up Appearances
Knight Rider
Laurel & Hardy Films
Life on Mars
Miami Vice
Morse
Mr Bean
~~Only Fools and Horses~~
Open All Hours
Starsky & Hutch
The Darling Buds of May
The Italian Job
The New Avengers
The Professionals
The Saint (1960s)
The Spy Who Loved me
The Sweeny
Z-Cars

63. HALF TIME QUIZ   TEAM NAME _____

These addresses are all famous. Some are fictitious, some are notorious criminals and some are historical or literary figures who used to live there. Who lives or lived at these addresses ? On some addresses clues are given to help you.

1.	13 Coronation Street, Weatherfield, Greater Manchester	
2.	742 Evergreen Terrace, Springfield, USA	
3.	39 Hilldrop Crescent, Camden Road, Holloway, London, (famous murderer caught in 1910)	
4.	32 Windsor Gardens, London (Children's character)	
5.	251 Menlove Avenue, Liverpool	
6.	30 Kelsall Street, Liverpool (sit-com family)	
7.	25 Cromwell Street, Gloucester	
8.	4 Privet Drive, Little Whinging, Surrey	
9.	11 Downing Street , Westminster, London (Government cabinet position)	
10.	62 West Wallaby Street, Wigan, Lancs	
11.	124 Conch Street, Bikini Bottom, Pacific Ocean	
12.	The Parsonage, Haworth, West Yorkshire	
13.	Oxenthorpe Road, Puddleby-on-the-Marsh, Slopshire, England (Doctor)	
14.	393 Old Commercial Road, Portsmouth, Hampshire	
15.	221B Baker Street, London	
16.	43b Albert Square, Walford, London (1991 to 2009)	
17.	24 Oil Drum Lane, Shepherd's Bush, London (Sit-com)	
18.	Number 1, London	
19.	Danemead, High Street, St Mary Mead	
20.	Southfork Ranch, Braddock County, Texas, USA	
21.	23 Railway Cuttings, East Cheam (Comedian)	
22.	Rydal Mount, Ambleside, Lake District	
23.	Wayne Manor, Gotham City, USA	
24.	10050 Cielo Drive , Beverly Hills, CA. (Famous murder)	
25.	19 Riverbank (Sit-com)	
26.	House-for-One, Toyland	
27.	Nelson Mandela House, Peckham, London	
28.	10 Rillington Place, Notting Hill, London	
29.	1600 Pennsylvania Avenue Northwest, Washington, D.C	
30.	344 Clinton St., Apt. 3B, Metropolis, USA	
31.	1313 Webfoot Walk, Duckburg, Calisota	

64. HALF TIME QUIZ TEAM NAME _____

This is all about famous crimes and criminals. Answer as many questions as you can

1.	In which month did the Great Train Robbery take place in 1963?	
2.	Which murderous family lived at '25 Cromwell Street'?	
3.	Near which town did Steve Wright commit 5 murders in 2006?	
4.	Who accidently murdered his children's nanny instead of his wife in 1974?	
5.	What is the name of the 8 yr old girl brutally murdered in 1867 whose name now stands for 'nothing of value'.	
6.	For what type of crime was Tom Keating well known?	
7.	How did George Smith murder his three wives between 1910 and 1915?	
8.	What was the name of the warehouse at Heathrow airport from which 3 tonnes of gold bullion was stolen in 1983?	
9.	What was Peter Sutcliffe's (Yorkshire Ripper) job or occupation?	
10.	How did John Haig dispose of his murder victims during the War?	
11.	Which Kent MP served an 18 month sentence for perjury in 1999?	
12.	Which 'Lord' was murdered on his boat in 1979 by the IRA?	
13.	The Stratton Brothers murdered a shop keeper in 1905, At their trial what kind of evidence was accepted for the first time in an English court?	
14.	Which former 'soap' actress was gangster Ronnie Knight married to?	
15.	Which murderer tried to escape to Canada with his girlfriend dressed as a boy on a liner in 1910?	
16.	Who was the last woman to be hanged in England in 1955?	
17.	What did Thomas Blood try to steal in 1671?	
18.	Who lived at '10 Rillington Place' and murdered 5 women there in the 50s?	
19.	What was Reggie and Ronnie Kray's older brother called?	
20.	Which of the McWhirter's (Ross or Norris), of 'Guinness Book of Records' fame, was murdered by the IRA in 1975 ?	
21.	Which King Edward was brutally murdered at Berkley Castle?	
22.	What was the name of the 10 yr old girl who murdered 2 toddlers in Newcastle in the 1960s?	
23.	In which part of London did Jack the Ripper murder his victims?	
24.	What was stolen from Westminster Abbey on Christmas Day in 1950?	
25.	How was Airey Neave MP murdered in 1979?	
26.	What was the name of the murdered 13 yr. old girl who has been at the centre of the recent 'phone hacking' enquiry?	

65. HALF TIME QUIZ TEAM NAME _____

How well do you know Britain's Motorways ? They rarely run into the heart of towns and cities so all you have to do is write the major town or city near to the start or end of the motorway. Look at the M2 as an example below. It doesn't matter which way round you've got the start and finish. Some answers are already filled in. There are some A roads to fill in too.

	M/way	Start	Finish
1.	M1		
2.	M2	Rochester	Faversham
3.	M3		
4.	M4		
5.	M5		
6.	M6	Rugby	
7.	M8		
8.	M9		Dunblane
9.	M11		
10.	M20	Swanley	
11.	M23	Caterham	
12.	M27		Southampton
13.	M40		
14.	M53	Birkenhead	
15.	M55		
16.	M62		
17.	M65	Burnley	
A Roads	~~~~~~~~~~~~~~	~~~~~~~~~~~~~~	
18.	A1	London	
19.	A3	London	
20.	A5	London	
21.	A10	London	
22.	A12	London	
23.	A13	London	
24.	A14	Rugby	

Source AA Road Atlas

66. HALF TIME QUIZ   TEAM NAME _____

You have to identify the country of origin for these major international companies. Most of these companies have interests in most major trading nations, but where were they set up originally.   EXAMPLE:-

Prada (Women's fashion)   *Italy*

1.	Brother (Office Equipment)	
2.	Carlsberg (Beer)	
3.	Daewoo (Cars & Electrical Products)	
4.	Dunlop (Tyres)	
5.	Durex (Condoms)	
6.	Elf (Oil & Petrol)	
7.	Esso (Oil & Petrol)	
8.	E-on (Energy Company)	
9.	Heinz (Food Products)	
10.	Hoover (Electrical Goods)	
11.	HSBC (Bank)	
12.	Hyundai (Cars)	
13.	Ikea (Furniture)	
14.	Johnson & Johnson (Medical Goods)	
15.	JVC (Electronic Goods)	
16.	Kodak (Photographic Goods)	
17.	Lacoste (Fashion Goods)	
18.	Lidl (Supermarket)	
19.	Lego (Children's building Materials)	
20.	Nestle (Confectionary & Food)	
21.	Nokia (Mobile Phones)	
22.	Olivetti (Electronic Goods)	
23.	O_2 (Mobile Phones)	
24.	Pfizer (Research & Drugs)	
25.	Philips (Electrical Goods)	
26.	Polydor (Record & CD Label)	
27.	Rolex (Watches)	
28.	Seat (Cars)	
29.	Shell (Oil & Petrol)	
30.	Skoda (Cars)	
31.	Siemens (Electrical Goods)	
32.	Stella Artois (Beer)	

67. HALF TIME QUIZ   TEAM NAME _____

The clues should lead you to the name of a type of sweet or chocolate bar or box, (many are brand names). All that is needed is the name of the item and nothing else.

For Example:-   Prisoner escape   *Breakaway*

1.	Royal jungle dweller's local	
2.	Birmingham suburb that's darker than most !	
3.	Reverend Geraldine's favourite bar	
4.	Princely game !	
5.	Public transport with stairs !	
6.	Commemorations of important events	
7.	Chocolate favoured by complete lunatics perhaps	
8.	Chinese ones can be misleading, especially in the spelling !	
9.	A single letter exchange leads you to lady's unmentionables !	
10.	They go well with the wine according to the old song	
11.	Pontefract's favourite	
12.	Often bought for romantic messages rather than the taste	
13.	Only fit for Kings and Emperors perhaps	
14.	Variety of ladies in the toy room	
15.	Membership unnecessary to enjoy this treat	
16.	A contradiction —— Chewy but crunchy	
17.	24 carat	
18.	Feline food minus the fifth letter of the alphabet	
19.	Fourth 'rock' out	
20.	Loot !	
21.	Sounds like they should come from a Med island	
22.	Like the Trevi but with powder	
23.	Dairy produce platter	
24.	A road of the best houses	
25.	Corn, wheat or bran, it doesn't matter, just one bit from the packet is enough	
26.	Stephen's Eastern Joys	
27.	Could this be Mr Walker's favourite when he worked for the BBC	
28.	Where the 'showbiz' people buy a drink	
29.	They're always top of the class	
30.	To confuse an issue	
31.	A place where calves may get a drink perhaps !	
32.	UFOs	

68. HALF TIME QUIZ   TEAM NAME _____

These clues should lead you to a song, tune or nursery rhyme with the name of an ANIMAL, that is a MAMMAL, REPTILE or AMPHIBIAN. No birds, insects, fish or other creatures are in the answers. All you need to do is to write down the name of the animal and nothing else. Example:-

<u>Mud</u> - dy dancing feet   *Tiger*

1.	"Loving would be easy if the colours were like my dreams" so sung George in '84	
2.	Bill and his cosmic group intended to return	
3.	The feline question of 1965. (Be precise in your answer !)	
4.	Mary's young follower	
5.	One of the eight that flies with SC in December	
6.	Rodent catching device, as sung about in '78	
7.	Question asked in 1953 about an animal in a shop display. (Be precise)	
8.	Neil Sedaka went like this in'59	
9.	Animal from 'Satan's home' according to this American singer in '93	
10.	A "boogie" song sung by Ella Fitzgerald in an Abbott & Costello film in 1942	
11.	It's napping this evening in the jungle	
12.	"I don't wanna be a tiger, cause tigers play too rough" what do I want to be ?	
13.	That annoying ringtone that made No1 in 2005	
14.	Mad animals according to Donnie & his brothers	
15.	Mud lover according to Michael & Donald's very old song	
16.	A whole load of supermarket chat !	
17.	Mr J and Suzie had so much fun in 1972	
18.	Sounds like this little animal's about to burst in the nursery	
19.	"Sitting on a cornflake, waiting for the van to come", What am I ?	
20.	There is one of these in most families somewhere, usually dark coloured	
21.	'Unseeing trio terrorise the lady of the house' !	
22.	According to the old song, one night, she packed up and left the circus	
23.	This young trio confessed to their mother that they had lost their gloves	
24.	Bill, Graeme and Tim's silly ape song of the 70's	
25.	'Paddy's pet causes havoc' !	
26.	Sounds like Duran Duran just wanted something to eat in '82	
27.	Stop this Aussie animal escaping, secure it well please	
28.	'Triplets outwit lupine character'	
29.	Tommy's little fellow who wanted to fight with the big ones in '59	
30.	Donnie's teenage emotions, nobody understands !	

69. HALF TIME QUIZ TEAM NAME _____

The clues should lead you to the name of a bird. All that is needed is the name of the bird and nothing else. For Example:-

	Marian's outlaw boyfriend	*Robin*
1.	Invaluable at the docks but more usually found wading and feeding elsewhere	
2.	The miner's friend	
3.	Poetic songbird that probably never did sing in London in wartime	
4.	Not the brightest spark, it can hide its head but predators can still see it	
5.	My grey-headed friend has a bad reputation. Lock up anything valuable.	
6.	According to Aesop this bird is a source of riches. Disposing of it would be foolish	
7.	Their name is the only link between a water bird and a fast locomotive	
8.	Six must remain in their special London home, or the Queen may loose her throne	
9.	Sheryl is still recording and touring after seventeen years	
10.	Said to be responsible for increasing the World's human population	
11.	Snake killer and quite useful in the office too.	
12.	Speedy fellow on the tarmac	
13.	Big Geoff's favourite bird	
14.	How would you like Rod's arm shoved up where an arm shouldn't go !	
15.	Spoken by Neil when he settled in a faraway spot	
16.	Jack sailed his ship and plundered in the western Atlantic	
17.	Said to vocalise tunefully before their demise	
18.	Parent company to B&Q & Screwfix among other retail outlets	
19.	Aussie actor, long since departed, best known for his hell-raising lifestyle	
20.	Never actually seen at Dover	
21.	On the board it can move in all directions except diagonally	
22.	Use a proper mallet you stupid girl and leave the hedgehogs alone as well	
23.	A clever friend of Christopher and Winnie	
24.	Two dozen prepared for consumption, sang when exposed	
25.	Said to bring luck, good or bad depending on numbers	
26.	In Roald's story this bird is useful in the window cleaning business	
27.	Richard Bach wrote about how Jonathan L. learnt to fly.	
28.	You could be reading a book and eating a snack, both with the same name	
29.	Enjoys laughing at Aussie jokes	
30.	A gold statuette of this bird leads to a 1941 Oscar winning adventure film	
31.	To be dead in this way is to never exist again	

70. HALF TIME QUIZ   TEAM NAME _____

These clues should lead you to a song title or tune with the name of a <u>colour</u> in it. All that is needed is the colour and nothing else. For Example:-

	Mr P's favourite footwear, no doubt	*Blue*
1.	Mr J says farewell to Dorothy's 'path'.	
2.	This girl is worth more than just a written down phone number	
3.	Fred was getting all dressed up with more than just a hat over 70 years ago	
4.	It sounds as if this female is going to take up boxing !	
5.	"Put wood in hole please ! " Mr Stevens	
6.	BC's best selling yuletide song	
7.	This feline character led to a number of successful films and an animated series	
8.	Somewhat unconventional underwater transport	
9.	It sounds like Jimi might have seen coloured mist, it's probably all in his mind really !!	
10.	ELO's happy song about a beautiful day	
11.	Snoopy's opponent in the 60s	
12.	A wartime success, pass the milk please !	
13.	A condemned man dreams of home and his girlfriend, Mary	
14.	Frank could have been singing about an ancient branded box of chocolates in 1961	
15.	In 2003 Dido had no intention of giving in	
16.	Swimming apparel that barely covers the essentials!	
17.	Aged rockers who may have done a bit of DIY when they were younger	
18.	It sounds like Crystal has had some kind of colour change to her irises !	
19.	Female 'quack doctor' dishing out strange drugs!	
20.	What Venus was wearing in 62	
21.	A very ancient but quite well known tune, possibly of Tudor origin	
22.	An ex-con is looking for a sign on a *Quercus.* No sign, then he will continue his journey	
23.	Those aged rockers (No.17) needed sweetening up in 71	
24.	London football club hit in 1972	
25.	Prince - ly precipitation	
26.	A Yuletide caribou	
27.	A good old Irish folk song about an apprentice betrayed by a colleen !	
28.	I would like to have seen T-Rex try to do this, poor bird !	
29.	Mr Morrison's good-looking girl friend.	
30.	A silly 1950s song by Mr Bygraves about a bathroom article	
31.	Mr P, when missing his girl, had a melancholy yuletide	
32.	Chris is in love with his dancing partner, 'love the dress' !	

71. HALF TIME QUIZ TEAM NAME _____

All the following answers contain the name of a **FLOWER**. You just have to find the name of the flower from the clues and nothing else.   For Example:-

Tiptoe through these in Holland!!   *Tulips*

No.	Clue	
1.	2004 film where sisters played by Judy Dench & Maggie Smith save a stranger found on a beach in Cornwall	
2.	Descending ice-crystals	
3.	Indian Princess from 'Neverland', kidnapped by Captain Hook	
4.	What grew "Between the crosses row on row" in 1915	
5.	Vulpine paw protectors	
6.	Highly scented flowers on a shrub called '*Lonicera*'. How sweet !!	
7.	Aquatic subject of many of Monet's later paintings	
8.	'Car Wash' singer	
9.	Reflect light on your chin to determine your love for a dairy product	
10.	2006 film, based on a notorious unsolved American murder, that starred Scarlett Johansson	
11.	Tree flower, purple or white, that symbolises "First Love"	
12.	Yellow favourites of Van Gogh	
13.	Controversial singer who released singles in 2009 called 'The Fear', 'Not Fair' and one with a title that cannot be included here !!!	
14.	'The shy girl left on her own at the dance'	
15.	"It's my sister ____?____. She's the one with the swimming pool, Mercedes and room for a pony"	
16.	Irish born female author who wrote 'The Sea The Sea' in 1978	
17.	Tree flowers, also a branded shoe polish	
18.	English flower name derived from the French for "Lions Tooth"	
19.	"Small & white, clean & bright"	
20.	Nancy 'took her seat' in 1919 — Nancy who ?	
21.	The story of a Jewish lady & her chauffer, filmed in 1989	
22.	'Mythical creature about to bite, perhaps' !!	
23.	'Always remembered'	
24.	Lent lily	
25.	Vanilla's flower family	
26.	Evora, Elite, Eclat, Esprite & Europa are all types of .... !	
27.	Source of saffron	

72. HALF TIME QUIZ   TEAM NAME _____

All the following clues lead to answers contain the name of a metal or metal alloy. You just have to find the metal from the clues and nothing else. No metals are repeated.   For Example:-

Eighties band, first chart hit in 1982 was 'Run to the Hills'   *Iron (Maiden)*

1.	Money !!	
2.	Comedian's bad joke — 'went down ....'	
3.	Low melting point alloy for circuit work !	
4.	Highly resistant light metal used widely in the modern aerospace industry	
5.	All that Freda Payne had left (In 1970)	
6.	Churchill wanted it for Spitfires.	
7.	1968 'Small Faces' song about a vertically challenged person	
8.	A high intake of this in mineral form is bad for cardiac health.	
9.	5c	
10.	Early 80s TV science fiction fantasy starring David McCallum	
11.	Reward for an artiste selling 600,000 singles in Britain	
12.	Outer coating in the galvanisation of ferrous metals	
13.	Shiny tap coating	
14.	Officer of the law !	
15.	Light the ribbon and produce 'white light' in the chemistry Lab !	
16.	Ancient alloy for tankards and other such objects	
17.	Dental filling alloy	
18.	Widely used to create electricity or possibly to 'blow up the World' !!	
19.	Kid's bone strengthener in food	
20.	Shiny, grey, nocturnal, half inch insects often found in homes	
21.	Element material for Edison & Swann's invention	
22.	The time when the Beaker People settled in Britain	
23.	K is the clue, essential for good health	
24.	Heavy metal named after a planet	
25.	Roman messenger of the Gods	
26.	Known as 'Red Brass' in America, this is an alloy of 4 metals with a name that reflects its original use in making firearms	
27.	The Victorians favourite poison	

73. HALF TIME QUIZ TEAM NAME _____

The clues should lead you to the name of a either a day or a month to be found in the title of a <u>song, book, TV programme, film or the name of a celebrity</u>. The D or M next to the question number indicates which it is. Just write down the month or day.

Example D   The Rats seem to hate it   *Monday*

1.M	Seasonal weather enjoyed by Disney's deer !	
2.D	Get the popcorn ready for a great night out, saves <u>drifting</u> about with nothing to do !	
3.M	Carol King's gloomy weather prediction	
4.D	Girl band formed in 2006, first single in 2008 'If this is Love'	
5.D	G K Chesterton — 'The man who was _____?_____'	
6.D	Mums & Dads '66 sad song	
7.D	'If it's ? it must be Belgium' , zany 1969 comedy film	
8.M	Mr John (not Elton!), notable artist and pacifist, needs his first name shortened slightly	
9.M	Busting out all over in Carousel	
10.D	Debbie 'knew a girl from a lonely street, cold as ice cream but still as sweet'	
11.D	The Gibb Brothers' rave up, perhaps making themselves ill !!	
12.D	Sillitoe's 1960 'kitchen sink' drama set in a Nottingham factory	
13.D	Bangles crazy day	
14.M	The Bee Gees 'were small and Christmas trees were tall' in '69	
15.D	The Easybeats were constantly thinking of this day	
16.D	1960 Greek film with a Oscar winning hit song	
17.D	S & G are about to leave in the 'small hours'. 1964 debut album.	
18.M	One of three presenters of the best known motoring programme	
19.M	Dot, who works in the laundrette !	
20.D	U2's commemoration of an event in N. Ireland	
21.M	A well remembered night in the 60s by 'winter, spring, summer etc.' !	
22.M	Anita Dobson's guitarist husband	
23.D	Marti Webb wishes to be told bad news only on this day at the zoo	
24.D	Wigfield's looking forward to a great night out !	
25.M	Favourite comedienne of 'Ad Fab' and 'Last of the Summer Wine'	
26.M	Barbara Dickson's two months (1980 hit), either will do !	
27.M	Frederic, an old time Hollywood actor, won 2 Oscars, and died in 1975 aged 77	
28.D	Stones, mardi rouge !!	
29.M	Pat Boone 1957 '? Love'	
30.D	1999 Bowie single lifted from his album 'Hours....'	
31.M	Sitcom (89 to 94) set in London about a widowed solicitor	

74. HALF TIME QUIZ   TEAM NAME _____

These clues should lead you to the name of a town or city (most are cities) anywhere in the World. You just have to identify the city the "thing" is in.

Ex.	The Little Mermaid statue	*Copenhagen*
1.	The Imperial Palace	
2.	The Willis Tower (Formally Sear's Tower)	
3.	Sagrada Família	
4.	Petronas Towers	
5.	The Spanish Riding School	
6.	Khalifa Tower (World's tallest building)	
7.	The Raffles Hotel	
8.	The Swiss Re Building (or Tower)	
9.	The Golden Temple (India)	
10.	Statue of Christ the Redeemer	
11.	The Great Pyramid	
12.	The International Court of Justice	
13.	Basilique du Sacré-Cœur	
14.	The Hermitage Museum	
15.	La Scala Opera House	
16.	St Mark's Campanile	
17.	Ha'penny Bridge (Not in England)	
18.	Shwedagon Pagoda	
19.	Soweto	
20.	Kowloon	
21.	Chrysler Building	
22.	The Pantheon	
23.	The Temple of Heaven	
24.	The Brandenburg Gate	
25.	The Smithsonian Museums	
26.	The HQ of 'The Red Cross'	
27.	The Charles Bridge	
28.	The CN Tower (Formally the World's tallest)	
29.	The Acropolis	
30.	Council of the European Union	
31.	Hagia Sophia (Former mosque, now a museum)	
32.	Fisherman's Wharf	

75. HALF TIME QUIZ   TEAM NAME _____

These clues should lead you to the name of a fruit, vegetable or herb. All you need to write down is the name of the fruit, veg or herb.   Example:-
Unpleasant appearance of something Tyson once bit off   *Cauliflower*

1.	Controversial film - a bit of a 'wind - up' really !	
2.	Steinbeck classic	
3.	Flightless bird with very clean shoes maybe !!	
4.	Lennon memorial in America	
5.	"Day - o !" Harry's song	
6.	Actor who escaped in 'drag' in a 1958 HOT film	
7.	Known for strengthening a sailor !	
8.	The third person in a relationship designed for two	
9.	Strange TV comedy character, hardly ever spoke !	
10.	Produced our best known spy on the silver screen	
11.	Quote—"Don't mention the War !"	
12.	'She's got the way to move me (and grove me)' so says Mr D	
13.	"Roll a bowl a ball a penny a pitch"	
14.	2008 movie that centres round a rare form of marijuana	
15.	MOVE to a fruity street !	
16.	Created for Nellie at The Savoy in 1892	
17.	The 'must-have' toy of '83. Not always considered to be attractive !	
18.	Baloo recommends Mowgli to pick this along with the prickly pear, according to Disney	
19.	The friendly old lion who lived in a garden with Bayleaf the gardener	
20.	A phantom one was around in Victorian London according to Mr B & Mr C in their show	
21.	One who is profoundly wise	
22.	Marvin & Tammi thought the World was a big one	
23.	The professor in a crime game	
24.	Cosmic transport !	
25.	'Hilly' hit for Fats Domino in'56. Also recorded by both Elvis and Cliff	
26.	'Bone juice' - popular with dogs and important to surgeons	
27.	'Son of my Father' 1972 hit	
28.	Dance craze of the early 60s	
29.	Polanski's 1968 horror film starring Mia Farrow. Strange events happen to a young couple	
30.	A station that may have been used by The Beatles or Ken Dodd at sometime	
31.	Euphemism for Dolly's outstanding features !	

76. HALF TIME QUIZ TEAM NAME _____

These clues should lead you to the name of a district of <u>LONDON</u>, a park, station or well known street.   For Example:-

Defended site with a pachyderm

Elephant & Castle

1.	The sleuth doctor's boss lived here	
2.	Ms Berresford's litterpickers lived here	
3.	The cheapest on the board	
4.	Seaside trench	
5.	Very famous street named after 'stiff collars with scalloped edges and lace'	
6.	The important lady who left her name all over the world including London	
7.	Very important road in London that's NOT full of shops !	
8.	Ornithologist's viewing street !	
9.	Helvetian abode	
10.	Where noblemen should be tried	
11.	Origin of most taxicab licenses	
12.	From Dorset town to theatre street	
13.	Large area for Stevenson's doctor's alter-ego	
14.	Famous for the 'Me and My Girl' walk	
15.	You were never alone with one in the 50s & 60s on this street	
16.	Yorkshire castle town = Thames side park	
17.	Viscount, Cavalier, Cresta, Wyvern, Velox, Victor, Viva, Senator, Carlton etc.	
18.	Similar name to Sevenoaks, different number—different tree	
19.	Get there <u>fast</u> with the news, or at least you used to !	
20.	The most notorious criminal's haunt	
21.	Lancelot's way over the water	
22.	Where Hugh and Julia first met and fell in love.	
23.	Paris has one too also in the middle of a large roundabout	
24.	Leona's joined by an amateur actor	
25.	Furious ruler	
26.	The finish of Coe's best known run	
27.	Tall narrow windbreak tree	
28.	Road for Michael, James or Basildon possibly	
29.	Eurovision's finest and best known song	
30.	Famous for its carbon crystals	
31.	Look here for the little chap possibly with orange jam on his face	
32.	A hunting cry	

77. HALF TIME QUIZ   TEAM NAME _____

The clues below should lead you to an answer containing the name of a compass direction, - NORTH, SOUTH, EAST or WEST, or a word containing a compass direction, eg. NORTHERN.

Ex.	Film	Disney film (1946) starring 'Uncle Remus'!	*Song of the South*
1.	US Army	He negotiated with the Contras in 1986, sacked by Reagan.	
2.	Film	(1937) One of Stan & Ollie's comic stories.	
3.	Boy Band	Irish—Managed by Louis Walsh, very successful.	
4.	Song	1978 hit by 'Renaissance'.	
5.	Film star	Born 1930. Once shared top billing with an orang-utan.	
6.	TV Program	Cult series featuring 'Stan, Kyle & Kenny'	
7.	Town	East Midlands—famous for footwear at one time	
8.	Country	African—Only became an independent country in 2011	
9.	Person	Notorious female criminal.	
10.	Island	British overseas territory, east of the Falkland Islands	
11.	Town	Essex resort	
12.	Film star	(1893—1980) 'Inflatable life jacket' !!!	
13.	Village	Devon. Famous for its exclamation mark !	
14.	Actor	British—Married to Prunella Scales	
15.	TV actor	'Batman' in the 60s	
16.	Boy Band	1994 number 1 hit 'Stay Another Day'	
17.	Fem. singer	'Modern Girl' and '9 to 5 (Morning Train)'	
18.	Dog	Of Scottish origin	
19.	Song	Pet Shop Boys 1984 Number 1 hit	
20.	Town	West Sussex—Famous hospital for treating burns patients	
21.	Film	The warring gangs of New York (1961)	
22.	Film	(1959) Directed by Hitchcock, starred Cary Grant	
23.	Band	Number 1 hit in 1990 with 'A Little Time'	
24.	Resort	Very close to Portsmouth	
25.	Film	James Dean—cult movie (1955)	
26.	TV Series	Featured a Canadian Mountie called Benton Fraser.	
27.	Country	Half an island, former Portuguese colony, near Indonesia.	
28.	TV Series	Famous ranch in a southern US state in a popular soap	
29.	Film	Rogers and Hammerstein's ocean tale, (1958)	
30.	Singer	(1970) - 'Games People Play'	
31.	US State	Bordered by Kentucky, Ohio, Pennsylvania & Maryland	

78. HALF TIME QUIZ TEAM NAME _____

These clues should lead to the name of an AMERICAN STATE. Some are direct or cryptic clues, some are anagrams and some are a play on words. All you have to do is find the State.

No.	Clue	
1.	The old one is in Southern England.	
2.	'Sonic wins' - no, not a winning horse, just a place that needs to be reorganised	
3.	Trumpeter Armstrong with some extra letters after his name.	
4.	Birthplace of BO	
5.	Adventurer, Mr Jones, took his dad on a crusade !	
6.	Mums and Dads dreamed about it, and the surfers loved the dames there !	
7.	In 1955 Mr Williams wrote a play about a cat that got hot paws.	
8.	What Mrs Doonican might have bought Val as a present.	
9.	Pussycat hit of 76.	
10.	Red hen.	
11.	With this girl on my mind, I might need to get the midnight train to - somewhere	
12.	Four letters, 2 V and 2 C.	
13.	The military man's favourite food.	
14.	Sara sank. Changing things might tell us where !	
15.	The Gibb Brothers were going back there in 67.	
16.	Sounds like - I will questioned the girl !!	
17.	Tom & Anna get together but are a little confused.	
18.	Ms. Woolf	
19.	Burton's chocolate chip biscuits.	
20.	Sounds like you had a garden tool for removing weeds !	
21.	A follows the initials of a southern English island.	
22.	Home of the girl who squashed a witch in an imaginary place.	
23.	DIY supplies supplier until 1999.	
24.	Insect terror for potato farmers.	
25.	The upper of two on the Atlantic seaboard.	
26.	Cleaning a vast amount of clothing !	
27.	Initially give Nigel & Sonia 'a break', and muck things up !!	
28.	6-5000	
29.	Moist Anne needs sorting out.	
30.	Mr Rodgers and Mr Hammerstein's first venture together into musical theatre.	
31.	Up to date Latin American country.	
32.	Song about a 1941 mining disaster sung by the brothers Gibb.	

79. HALF TIME QUIZ   TEAM NAME _____

These clues should lead you to an item that you should find in a <u>SCHOOL</u>. Most are straight forward clues, but some are a play on words. Just write the item down and nothing else.

Example:- Sign-on at the surgery   *Register*

1.	What a fraudster may try to cook !	
2.	The nation's favourite sport.	
3.	Modern device to take the hard work out of sums.	
4.	Eyeholes	
5.	Where the men in white coats can be found !	
6.	1993 film about a mute woman, set in New Zealand in 1850	
7.	A vote for the farm vehicle to measure a turn.	
8.	Where Mrs Worthington's daughter should not be put !	
9.	Slim-fitting narrow skirt	
10.	A word from Hemmingway's novel's title, set in the Spanish Civil War.	
11.	1973 film starring Ryan O'Neil and his 10 year old daughter.	
12.	Needed to help draw Joseph's coat.	
13.	Branded Highland tipple !	
14.	Rolltop, Pedestal and Slant-Top	
15.	Whacko ! Jimmy Edward's part in this very old sit-com.	
16.	Invaluable device invented in 1959 by the X... Company.	
17.	What the kid's don't do at school and moan about !	
18.	Rock of South-East England	
19.	Lexicographer's tome.	
20.	Keep-fitter's favourite haunt.	
21.	Edward's hand substitutes, in the film !	
22.	Wire to stop sheets from separating.	
23.	Metal devices used to fix sleepers to rails.	
24.	2007 'Golden' fantasy-adventure film starring Nicole Kidman.	
25.	Ms Wood's TV sit-com (1998—2000)	
26.	Depositary used by theatre-goers when they first get there.	
27.	Lady swan	
28.	Shakespeare's theatre	
29.	Likely to be the noisiest place !	
30.	Condom colloquialism !	
31.	Monarch	

80. HALF TIME QUIZ TEAM NAME _____

These clues should lead you to an item or items that you should find in a
<u>HOSPITAL</u>. Some of them are anagrams and some are direct clues. Just write the
item down.

Example:-   What sailors call a sail   *Sheet*

1.	Large tropical eastern Atlantic shark	
2.	It's time the 'term theorem' detected a little heat.	
3.	The Royal Tabor is where to find the people in white.	
4.	Red rugs hold the answer!	
5.	Colonel who tried to steal the Crown Jewels.	
6.	Some drab filter oil will get the rhythm right again with a little tweaking!	
7.	Electoral districts of towns or cities.	
8.	Eric Charles Gill starts to get to the heart of the problem !	
9.	Sounds like a card game for one !	
10.	One of life's essentials can be bottled but is also freely available around you.	
11.	Spouse that is neither too tall or small.	
12.	Mummy's apparel.	
13.	Ideal vessel for those who like to cook while sleeping !	
14.	The home of herbaceous flowers.	
15.	Sounds like the caviar fish who has no tea !	
16.	R.Saxy must be organised properly.	
17.	One of many to the west of IOW.	
18.	A dark beer made from charred malt.	
19.	The recipient of Kenneth Williams's Oooooo !	
20.	French wall-slap!	
21.	The vehicle Judy sang in, in 'Meet me in St Louis'	
22.	Inspector Tie is probably the first person you'll meet.	
23.	What Moses supposedly brought down from Sinai.	
24.	Doris Day kind of talk with Rock Hudson.	
25.	Who has been on TV since 63. This is a statement not a question.	
26.	Deranged toe step cosh is used to hear those delicate sounds.	
27.	Mr Sinatra faced a final one in his song!	
28.	The place to get your curing chemicals.	
29.	Piston pump!	
30.	The home of drama.	
31.	Bug killer on a grand scale.	

ANSWERS

1. **OSCAR WINNING SONGS** 1. The Way You Look Tonight, 2. Over the Rainbow 3. When you Wish Upon a Star 4. White Christmas 5. Swingin' on a Star 6. Zip-a-dee-doo-dah 7. Do not Forsake me oh my Darling 8. Secret Love 9. What ever will be will be (Que sera sera) 10. Moon River 11. Chim chim cher-ee 12. Talk to the Animals 13. Windmills of my Mind 14. Raindrops Keep Falling on my Head 15. Up Where we Belong 16. What a Feeling 17. I Just Called to Say I Love You 18. Take my Breath Away 19. I've Had the Time of my Life 20. Under the Sea 21. A Whole New World 22. Streets of Philadelphia 23. Can you Feel the Love Tonight 24. My Heart Will Go on 25. Jai Ho

2. **REAL NAMES** 1. Tony Curtis 2. Eminem 3. John Wayne 4. Danny Kaye 5. Fats Domino 6. Barbara Windsor 7. Bob Dylan 8. Buddy Holly 9. Ringo Starr 10. Judy Garland 11. Sigourney Weaver 12. Michael Caine 13. Richard E Grant 14. Fatboy Slim 15. Cilla Black 16. Lulu 17. Doris Day 18. Elton John 19. Noddy Holder 20. Sting 21. Englebert Humperdinck 22. Cary Grant 23. Marilyn Monroe 24. Big Daddy 25. Lionel Bart.
The 5 real names are:- Matt Damon, Johnny Depp, Neil Diamond, Clint Eastwood & Anthony Hopkins

3. **SIT-COM STARS** 1. Robert Lindsey & Zoe Wannamaker 2. Richard Wilson & Annette Crosby 3. John Thaw 4. Penelope Keith & Peter Bowles 5. Wilfred Pickles & Irene Handl 6. Leonard Rossiter 7. Patricia Routledge 8. Thora Hird 9. James Bolem & Rodney Bewes 10. Bill Maynard 11. Geoffrey Palmer & Judi Dench 12. John Cleese & Prunella Scales 13. Donald Sinden & Windsor Davies 14. Wendy Craig & Geoffrey Palmer 15. Nicholas Lyndhurst 16. Ronnie Barker & David Jason 17. Stephanie Cole & Graham Crowden 18. Paul Eddington & Nigel Hawthorne 19. Richard Briars 20. Harry H Corbett & Wilfred Bramble 21. Brian Murphy & Yootha Joyce 22. Jimmy Jewel & Hylda Baker 23. Nicholas Lyndhurst & Celia Imrie 24. Anton Rogers

4. **CHILD ACTORS** 1. Jenny Agguter 2. Drew Barrymore 3. Freddy Bartholomew 4. Jamie Bell 5. Jackie Coogan 6. Macaulay Culkin 7. Karan Dotrice 8. Jody Foster 9. Judy Garland 10. Rupert Grint 11. Scarlett Johansson 12. Kiera Knightley 13. Bonnie Langford 14 Ramona Marquez 15. Mark Lester 16. Lindsey Lohan 17. Hayley Mills 18. Anthony Newley 19. Tatum O'Neal 20. River Phoenix 21. Daniel Radcliffe 22. Micky Rooney 23. Winona Ryder 24. Elizabeth Taylor 25. Shirley Temple 26. Emma Watson 27. Jack Wild 28. Mara Wilson 29. Natalie Wood

5. **OSCARS, BEST FILM 1935-1976** 1. Mutany on the Bounty 2. Gone With the Wind 3. Rebecca 4. Mrs Miniver 5. Casablanca 6. Hamlet 7. All About Eve 8. An American in Paris 9. The Greatest Show on Earth 10. From Here to Eternity 11. On the Waterfront 12. Marty 13. Around the World in 80 Days 14. The Bridge on the River Kwai 15. Gigi 16. Ben Hur 17. The Apartment 18. West Side Story 19. Lawrence of Arabia 20. Tom Jones 21. My Fair Lady 22. The Sound of Music 23. A Man for all Seasons 24. In the Heat of the Night 25. Oliver 26. Midnight Cowboy 27. Patton 28. The French Connection 29. The Godfather 30. The Sting 31. The Godfather: Part 2 32. One Flew Over the Cuckoo's Nest 33. Rocky

6. **OSCARS, BEST FILM 1978-2010** 1. The Deer Hunter 2. Kramer Verses Kramer 3. Ordinary People 4. Chariots of Fire 5. Gandhi 6. Terms of Endearment 7. Amadeus 8. Out of Africa 9. Platoon 10. The Last Emporer 11. Rain Man 12. Driving Miss Daisy 13. Dances With Wolves 14. The Silence of the Lambs 15. Unforgiven 16. Schlindler's List 17. Forrest Gump 18. Braveheart 19. The English Patient 20. Titanic 21. Shakespeare in Love 22. American Beauty 23. Gladiator 24. A Beautiful Mind 25. Chicago 26. The Lord of the Rings: The Return of the King 27. Million Dollar Baby 28. Crash 29. The Departed 30. No Country for Old Men 31. Slumdog Millionaire 32. The Hurt Locker 33 The King's Speech

7.   <u>ONE WORD FILM TITLES</u>   1. Alien   2. Big   3. Braveheart   4. Carrie   5. Chicago   6. Dracula   7. Exodus   8. Fame   9. Ghost   10. Gladiator   11. Hamlet   12. Iris   13. Jaws   14. Kes   15. Loot   16. Metropolis 17. Notorious 18. Oklahoma   19. Platoon   20. Papillion   21. Quadraphenia   22. Rebecca   23. Stagecoach   24. Sparticus 25. Tootsie   26. Unforgiven   27. Vertigo   28. Waterworld   29. X-Men   30.Yentl   31. Zulu

8.   <u>ANIMALS IN FILMS & TV</u>   1. Parrot   2. Dog (Border Collie)   3. Lobster   4. Owl (Snowy)   5. Killer Whale (Orca)   6. Elephant   7. Orang-Utang   8. Owl   9. Penguin   10. Pig   11. Otter   12. Dog   13. Leopard   14. Clown Fish   15. Rat   16. Duck   17. Seagull   18. Dolphin   19. Monkey   20. Wart Hog   21. Parrot   22. Mouse   23. Horse   24. Cat   25. Mouse   26. Woolley Mammoth   27. Ant   28. Dog (Spaniel)   29. Eagle   30. Chimpanzee   31. Parrot   32. Horse

9.   <u>TV CATCHPHRASES</u>   1. A silly moo   2. Monty Python ('s Flying Circus)   3. Kenny Everett   4. Lauren Cooper   5. It's good but it's not right   6. Larry Grayson   7. Play Your Cards Right   8. Blockbusters   9. Albert Steptoe   10. Michael Barrymore   11. Naff (off)   12. Bus Fare Home   13. You are awful but I like you   14. Matt Lucas   15. The Crystal Maze   16. Ali G   17. The War   18. Shut Up   19. John Virgo   20. Those fingers   21. Going for Gold   22. Jim (vicar of Dibley)   23. Blind Date   24. Cunning plan   25. Suits you Sir   26. Listen very carefully I shall say this only once   27. The Rise and Fall of Reginald Perrin   28. Onslow (keeping Up Appearances)

10.   <u>MUSICALS (MATCH)</u>   1. Zip-a-Dee-Doo-Dah   2. Ding Dong the Witch is Dead   3. Give a Little Whistle   4. The Lambeth Walk   5. Secret Love   6. Make 'em Laugh   7. Who Wants to be a Millionaire   8. Oh What a Beautiful Morning   9. Sit Down You'll Rocking the Boat   10. You'll Never Walk Alone   11. March of the Siamese Children   12. Happy Talk   13. America   14. Seventy-Six Trombones   15. Bachelor Boy   16. If I Were a Rich Man   17. I Could Have Danced All Night   18. Feed the Birds   19. The Bare Necessities   20. Me Ol' Bamboo   21. Willkommen   22. Consider Yourself   23. I Don't Know how to Love Him   24. Hopelessly Devoted to You   25.Good Morning Starshine   26. Hakuna Matata   27. Oh What a Circus   28. A Whole New World   29. The Music of the Night   30. Like a Virgin   31. Razzle Dazzle   32. Our Last Summer

11.   <u>DISNEY FILM CHARACTERS</u>   1. Robin Hood   2. The Aristocats   3. Beauty and the Beast   4. Pocahontas   5. The Little Mermaid   6. 101 Dalmatians   7. Cinderella   8. Sleeping Beauty   9. The Lion King   10. Snow White and the Seven Dwarfs   11. The Hunchback of Notre Dame   12. Pinocchio   13. Alice in Wonderland   14. Dumbo   15. The Jungle Book   16. Fantasia   17. Aladdin   18. The Sword in the Stone   19. Peter Pan   20 Mulan   21. Bambi   22. The Lady and the Tramp   23. Hercules   24. The Rescuers   25. Winnie the Pooh

12.   <u>FAMOUS QUOTES FROM FILMS</u>   1. Dirty Harry   2. Dirty Dancing   3. Love Story   4. Casablanca   5. Rebecca   6. Forrest Gump   7. Pirates of the Caribbean   8. All About Eve   9. The Shining   10. Gone With the Wind   11. Singin' in the Rain   12. My Fair Lady   13. Bonnie & Clyde   14. Titanic   15. On the Waterfront   16. When Harry met Sally   17. A Night at the Opera   18. Doctor Strangelove   19. The Godfather   20. Notting Hill   21. King Kong   22. Terminator 2   23. Finding Nemo   24. The Wizard of Oz   25. Starwars   26. Alien

13.   <u>JAMES BOND FILM THEMES (MATCH)</u>   1. Matt Monroe   2. Shirley Bassey   3. Tom Jones   4. Nancy Sinatra   5. Louis Armstrong   6. Shirley Bassey   7. Paul McCartney & Wings   8. Lulu   9. Carly Simon   10. Shirley Bassey   11. Sheena Easton   12. Rita Coolidge   13. Duran Duran   14. A-Ha   15. Gladys Knight   16. Tina Turner   17. Sheryl Crow   18. Garbage   19. Madonna   20. Chris Cornell   21. Jack White & Alicia Keys   22. Adele   23. Herb Alpert   24. Lani Hall

14.   <u>FILMS FROM INITIALS</u>   1. Top Hat   2. Bringing Up Baby   3. Gone With the Wind   4. Rebecca   5. Casablanca   6. Brief Encounter   7. Adam's Rib   8. Sunset Boulevard   9. Singin' in the Rain   10. High Noon   11. From Here to Eternity   12. Rebel Without a Cause   13. Psycho   14. Breakfast at Tiffany's   15. Move Over Darling   16. Viva Las Vegas   17. Doctor Zhivago   18. The Graduate   19. Bonnie & Clyde   20. Annie Hall   21. The French Lieutenant's Woman   22. Fatal Attraction   23. A Fish Called Wanda   24. Ghost   25. Pretty Woman   26. The Silence of the Lambs   27. Basic Instinct   28. Sleepless in Seattle   29. Moulin Rouge   30. Lost in Translation   31 Harry Potter and the Order of the Phoenix   32. The Curious Case of Benjamin Button   33. The King's Speech

15. <u>FILM PLACES</u>   1. A museum   2. A hotel   3. The Jury room at a court   4. A cafe   5. A Prison (devil's Island)   6. A World War 2 Bomber   7. A mobile hospital   8. A school   9. A railway station   10. A Japanese POW camp   11. A bank   12. A liner (ship)   13. A farm   14. Inside a human body   15. A psychiatric hospital   16. An ex-London Bus   17. A train   18. A Naval ship   19. A prison   20. A Mexican village   21. A hotel   22. A courtroom   23. A theatre / ballet school   24. A factory   25. A palace   26. A river boat   27. A motel   28. A school   29. A university (Havard)   30. A TV studio   31. A spaceship

16. <u>CHRISTMAS SONGS</u>   1. Bing Crosby   2. Judy Garland   3. Spike Jones   4. Gene Autry   5. Perry Como   6. Eartha Kitt   7. Elvis Presley   8. Brenda Lee   9. Dean Martin   10. Nat King Cole   11. Andy Williams   12. John & Yoko   13. Wizzard   14. Elton John   15. Slade   16. Mud   17. Chris De Burgh   18. Mike Oldfield   19. Greg Lake   20. Bing Crosby & David Bowie   21. Paul McCartney   22. Jona Lewie   23. The Waitresses   24. The Beach Boys   25. Wham   26. Band Aid   27. Aled Jones   28. Pogues & Kirsty McColl   29. Chris Rea   30. Cliff Richard   31. Mariah Carey

17. <u>BIRTH COUNTRIES</u>   1. Switzerland   2. Russia (Belarus today)   3. Canada   4. Australia   5. Ireland   6. Canada   7. Italy   8. New Zealand   9. Spain   10. Cuba   11. Argentina   12. Belgium   13. New Zealand   14. Jamaica   15. Ireland   16. Georgia (then USSR)   17. Zanzibar (Tanzania)   18. India   19. Australia   20. Australia   21. Cyprus   22. South Africa   23. Barbados   24. Portugal   25. Austria   26. Egypt   27. Denmark   28. South Africa   29. France   30. Belgium   31. Germany

18. <u>FILM REMAKES</u>   1. The Flight of the Phoenix   2. The Fly   3. King Kong   4. The Lady Vanishes   5. Planet of the Apes   6. 101 Dalmatians   7. The Nutty Professor   8. The thirty-nine steps   9. True Grit   10. Straw Dogs   11. The Parent Trap   12. The Italian Job   13. The Day the Earth Stood Still   14. A Nightmare on Elm Street   15. Ocean's Eleven   16. The Thomas Crown Affair   17. Psycho   18. Alice in Wonderland   19. Alfie   20. The Poseiden Adventure   21. Casino Royale

19. <u>HITS IN YEARS ENDING IN 0</u>   1. Cathy's Clown, The Everly Brothers   2. It's Now or Never , Elvis Presley   3. Apache, The Shadows   4. My Old Man's a Dustman, Lonnie Donegan   5. In the Summertime, Mungo Jerry   6. Wandering Star, Lee Marvin   7. Bridge Over Troubled Water, Simon & Garfunkel   8. Band of Gold, Freda Payne   9. Don't Stand so Close to me, The Police   10. No One Quite Like Grandma, St Winifred's School Choir   11, Super Trouper, Abba   12. The Tide is High, Blondie   13. Vogue, Madonna   14. A Little Time, The Beautiful South   15. Saviour's Day, Cliff Richard   16. Ice Ice Baby, Vanilla Ice   17. Breathless, The Corrs   18. Life is a Rollercoaster, Ronan Keating   19. Oops I did it Again, Britney Spears   20. Can We Fix it, Bob the Builder   21. Heroes, The X Factor Finalists   22. Bad Romance, Lady Gaga   23. When we Collide, Matt Cardle   24. California Gurls, Katie Perry & Snoop Dog

20. <u>HITS IN YEARS ENDING IN 3</u>   1. I Believe, Frankie Laine   2. She Wears Red Feathers, Guy Mitchell, 3. Answer Me, David Whitfield   4. How Much is That Doggie in the Window, Lita Roza   5. From me to You, The Beatles   6. Devil in Disguise, Elvis Presley   7. I Like it, Gerry & the Pacemakers   8. The Wayward Wind, Frank Ifield   9. Blockbuster, Sweet   10. Can the Can, Suzi Quatro   11. The Twelfth of Never, Donny Osmond   12. Get Down, Gilbert O'Sullivan   13. Uptown Girl, Billy Joel   14. Only You, Flying Pickets   15. Wherever I Lay my Hat, Paul Young   16. Karma Chameleon, Culture Club   17. I'd do Anything for Love, Meat Loaf   18. Pray, Take That   19. Young at Heart, The Bluebells   20. Mr Blobby, Mr Blobby   21. Leave Right Now, Will Young   22. Where is the Love, Black Eyed Peas   23. Mandy, Westlife   24. Spirit in the Sky, Gareth Gates & The Kumars

21. <u>HITS IN YEARS ENDING IN 4</u>   1. Secret Love, Doris Day   2. Cara Mia, David Whitfield   3. Three Coins in a Fountain, Frank Sinatra   4. Oh Mein Papa, Eddie Calvert   5. The House of the Rising Sun, The Animals   6. I Feel Fine, The Beatles   7. I'm into Something Good, Herman's Hermits   8. Have I the Right, The Honeycombs   9. She, Charles Aznavour   10. Love me for a Reason, The Osmonds   11. Gonna Make you a Star, David Essex   12. Sugar Baby Love, The Rubettes   13. I Just Called to Say I Love You, Stevie Wonder   14. The Power of Love, Frankie Goes to Hollywood   15. Freedom, Wham   16. Do They Know it's Christmas, Band Aid   17. Love is all Around, Wet Wet Wet   18. Saturday Night, Whigfield   19. Without You, Mariah Carey   20. Everything Changes, Take That   21. Radio, Robbie Williams   22. I'll Stand by You, Girls Aloud   23. Just Loose it, Emminem   24. Mysterious Girl, Peter Andre

22.   <u>CHART RECORDS</u>   1. I Believe, Frankie Laine   2. Unchained Melody, Jimmy Young   3. My Old Man's a Dustman, Lonnie Donegan   4. She Loves You, The Beatles   5. Tears, Ken Dodd   6. Mac Arthur Park, Richard Harris   7. Mull of Kintyre, Wings   8. A Little Peace, Nicole   9. You'll Never Walk Alone, The Crowd   10. Everything I do, Bryan Adams   11. Wannabe, Spice Girls   12. Candle in the Wind, Elton John   13. My Heart Will go on, Celine Dion   14. Believe, Cher   15. Can we Fix it, Bob the Builder   16. One Night, Elvis Presley

23.   <u>MUSIC COVERS FROM FILMS</u>   1. White Christmas   2. True Love   3. On the Street Where You Live   4. As Long as he Needs me   5. Til There Was You   6. If I Ruled the World   7. You'll Never Walk Alone   8. If I were a Rich Man   9. Edelweiss   10. Big Spender   11. America   12. Aquarius OR Let the Sun Shine in   13. I Don't Know How to Love Him   14. All That Jazz   15. Don't Cry for me Argentina   16. Hopelessly Devoted to You   17. Summer Nights OR You're the One That I Want   18. Memory   19. Happy Talk   20. All I ask of You   21. Love Changes Everything   22. Somewhere Over the Rainbow   23. The Circle of Life OR Can You Feel the Love Tonight   24. Somewhere   25. No Matter What

24.   <u>NOVELTY SONGS (MATCH)</u>   1. Joe Dolce   2. Allan Sherman   3. Royal Guardsmen   4. Chuck Berry   5. C W McCall   6. Benny Hill   7. Lonnie Donegan   8. Pat Boone   9. Harry Belafonte   10. Bobby Pickett   11. Crazy Frog   12. Bernard Cribbins   13. The Scaffold   14. Lita Roza   15. Napoleon XIV   16. Terry Scott   17. Flanders & Swann   18. Spitting Image   19. Monty Python   20. Brian Hyland   21. Peter Sellers   22. Sheb Woolley   23. Frankie Howerd   24. Ray Stevens   25. Charlie Drake

25.   <u>INSTRUMENTAL HITS</u>   1. Oh Mein Papa   2. Cherry Pink and Apple Blossom White   3. Poor People of Paris   4. Hoots Mon   5. Side Saddle   6. Wonderland by Night   7. Apache   8. Moon River   9. Take Five   10. The Stripper   11. Stranger on the Shore   12. Midnight in Moscow   13. Wonderful Land   14. Telstar   15. Nut Rocker   16. Green Onions   17. Wipe Out   18. A Walk in the Black Forest   19. Cast Your Fate to the Wind   20. Zorba's Dance   21. Spanish Flea   22. I Was Kaiser Bill's Batman   23. The Good, the Bad and the Ugly   24. Classical Gas   25. Albatross   26. Mouldy Old Dough   27. Amazing Grace   28. Popcorn   29. The Entertainer   30. Eye Level   31. The Floral Dance   32. Chariots of Fire

26.   <u>FIVE SINGERS</u>   1. New Jersey   2. Ava Gardner   3. High Society   4. Reprise   5. My Way   6. 1935   7. Sun Records   8. Heartbreak Hotel   9. A Little Less Conversation   10. Lisa Marie   11. Cardiff   12. Big Spender   13. Moonraker   14. Peter Finch   15. The Queen's Jubilee Concert   16. False   17. You Can Keep Your Hat on   18. Thunderball   19. Once   20. OBE   21. Like a Virgin   22. Evita   23. Beautiful Stranger   24. Guy Ritchie   25. Malawi

27.   <u>SONG LYRICS</u>   1. The White Cliffs of Dover   2. Everything I do   3. God Save the Queen   4. It's a Long Long Way to Tipperary   5. You'll Never Walk Alone   6. Hallelujah   7. We'll Meet Again   8. Abide With me   9. Bridge Over Troubled Water   10. Jerusalem   11. Imagine   12. Bohemian Rhapsody   13. My Way   14. White Christmas   15. Land of Hope and Glory   16. Rule Britannia   17. Candle in the Wind (1997)   18. Downtown   19. Dancing Queen

28.   <u>OPENING LYRICS</u>   1. King of the Road   2. I'm a Believer   3. These Boots are Made for Walkin'   4. Waterloo Sunset   5. All You Need is Love   6. Annie's Song   7. Stand by Your Man   8. Mama Mia   9. Don't Cry for me Argentina   10. Love me for a Reason   11. Dancing in the Street   12. Making Your Mind Up   13. Billie Jean   14. Karma Chameleon   15. Careless Whisper   16. Everything I do   17. I Will Always Love You   18. Love is All Around   19. Stay Another Day   20. Wannabe   21. Oops I Did it Again   22. Rock DJ   23. It's Raining Men   24. Leave Right Now   25. You Raised Me Up

29   <u>ADVERTS</u>   1. Qualcast mower   2. Dye her hair with Clairol   3. Llyles Golden Syrup   4. Snap, Crackle & Pop   5. Michael Parkinson   6. 118 118   7. Yellow Pages   8. Gold blend coffee   9. John Lewis   10. Zanussi   11. American Express   12. Strand   13. KFC   14. Colgate toothpaste   15. Carnation Milk   16. The Independent   17. Courage   18. Priviledge   19. Orson Welles   20. A Simples Life   21. Smarties   22. Andrex toilet roll

30. <u>PEOPLE WHO DIED IN 2011</u>   1. Severiano Ballerteros   2. Trevor Bannister   3. John Barry   4. Osama Bin Laden   5. Janet Brown   6. Henry Cooper   7. David Croft   8. Betty Driver   9. Peter Falk   10. Betty Ford   11. Joe Frazier   12. Muammer Gaddafi   13. Jet Harris   14.Steve Jobs   15. Kim Jong-il   16. Dick King Smith   17. Ted Lowe   18. Gary Mason   19. Ginger McCain   20. Pete Postlethwaite   21. Gerry Rafferty   22. Cliff Robertson   23. Jane Russell   24. Ken Russell   25. Jimmy Savile   26. Gary Speed   27. Eddie Stobart   28. Elizabeth Taylor   29. Amy Winehouse   30. Susannah York

31   <u>MUSIC WRITERS</u>   1. Claude Debussey   2. Thomas Arne   3. Johann Strauss   4. John-Philip Sousa   5. Paul Anka   6. Leonard Bernstein   7. Richard Rogers (Rogers & Hammerstein)   8. George   9. Irving Berlin   10. Tony Hatch   11. Lowe   12. Bacharach   13. Lloyd-Webber   14. King   15. Elton John   16. Dolly Parton   17. False   18. False   19. True   20. Bob Dylan   21. Holland   22. Gary Barlow   23. Leonard Cohen

32.   <u>DUETS</u>   1. Jennifer Warnes, (I've Had) the Time of my Life   2. Olivia Newton-John, You're the one that I want   3. Tammy Terrell, The Onion Song   4. Mel C, When You're Gone   5. Barbara Streisand, You Don't Bring me Flowers   6. Kiki Dee, Don't go Breaking My Heart   7. Jane Birkin, Je t'aime ... moi non plus   8. Nicole Kidman, Something Stupid   9. Jennifer Warnes, Up Where we Belong   10. Natalie Cole, Unforgettable   11. Bonnie Tyler, A Rockin' Good Way   12. Celine Dion, Immotality   13. Kylie Minogue, Especially For You   14. Lulu, Relight My Fire   15. Kim Weston, It Takes Two   16. Dolly Parton, Islands in the Stream   17. Aretha Franklin, I Knew You Were Waiting (for me)   18. Dusty Springfield, What Have I Done to Deserve This   19. Marie Osmond, I'm Leaving it All up to You   20. Kirsty McCall, Fairytale of New York

33.   <u>OLYMPICS 2012</u>   1. Road cycling   2. Volleyball   3. Rowing   4. Boxing   5. Equestrian   6. Mountain bike cycling   7. Road cycling time trial   8. Beach volleyball   9. 10km swimming   10. Canoe slalom   11. Archery   12. Gymnastics (artistic)   13. BMX cycling   14. Shooting   15. Football   16. Badminton   17. Sailing   18. Tennis   <u>The Opening Ceremony</u> 7 Olympians:- Duncan Goodhew, Kelly Holmes, Shirley Robinson, Daley Thompson, Lynn Davies, Mary Peters, & Steve Redgrave   7. Kenneth Branagh   8. The Arctic Monkeys   9. Bradley Wiggins   10. J K Rowling   <u>The Torch Relay</u> 1. 8000   2. Aluminium   3. Lands End   <u>Extra Q</u>   1. Third   2. The Who   3. Prince Harry

34.   <u>OLYMPIC VENUES & ATHLETES</u>   <u>Years</u> 48-London, 52-Helsinki 56-Melbourne 60-Rome   64-Tokyo 68 Mexico City 72-Munich 76-Montreal 80-Moscow 84-Los Angeles 88-Seoul   92-Barcelona 96-Atlanta 2000-Sydney 04-Athens 08-Beijing 12-London 16-Rio De Janeiro   20-Tokyo   <u>Questions</u> 1. Paris (1900 & 1924)   2. Terrorist attack that killed 11 Israeli athletes   3. A protest against the invasion of Afghanistan by the USSR   4. They made a political gesture supporting 'Black Power' rights when being awarded their medals.   <u>Athletes</u>   1. Long jump   2. 5000 & 10000m   3. Heptathlon   4. Triathlon   5. Boxing   6. Cycling   7. Shooting   8. Cycling   9. Sailing   10. Boxing   11. Canoeing   12. Taekwondo

35.   <u>SPORTS VENUES ETC.</u>   1. Birmingham   2. Liverpool   3. Edinburgh   4. Edinburgh   5. Glasgow   6. Stoke-on-Trent   7. Dumfries   8. London   9. Perth   10. Birkenhead   11. Shooting   12. Polo   13. Cricket OR Rugby   14. Showjumping   15. Football   16. Horse Racing   17. Rugby   18. Tennis   19. Motor Racing   20. Golf   21. Squash   22. Snooker   23. Horse Racing (jockey)   24. Figure skating   25. Darts

36.   <u>FOOTBALL CLUBS & MANAGERS</u>   1. Sunderland   2. Everton   3. Craven Cottage   4. The Valley   5. Aston Villa   6. Elland Road   7. Tottenham Hotspur   8. Liverpool   9. Stamford Bridge   10. Glasgow Rangers   11. The Magpies   12. The Blues   13. The Potters   14. The Pilgrims   15. The Seagulls   16. The Blades   17. The Reds   18. The Canaries   19. The Red Devils   20. The Hammers   MANAGERS   1. Alf Ramsey   2. Joe Mercer   3. Don Revie   4. Ron Greenwood   5. Bobby Robson   6. Graham Taylor   7. Terry Venables   8. Glenn Hoddle   9. Howard Wilkinson   10. Kevein Keegan   11. Peter Taylor   12. Sven-Goran Eriksson   13. Steve McClaren   14. Fabio Capello   15. Stuart Pearce   16. Roy Hodgson

37.   <u>DOG BREEDS</u>   1. St Bernard   2. Dachshunt   3. West Highland Terrier   4. Beagle   5. Rhodesian Ridgeback   6. Bichon Frisé   7. Staffordshire Bull Terrier   8. Rottweiler   9. King Charles Spaniel   10. Boxer   11. Jack Russell Terrier   12. Schnauzer   13. Whippet   14. Pug   5. Newfoundland   16. Skye Terrier   17. Afghan Hound   18. (Welsh) Corgi   19. Chow chow   20. Doberman Pinscher   21. Shih Tzu   22. Dalmatian   23. Bedlington Terrier   24. German Shepherd   25. Labrador (Retriever) 26. (English) Bulldog   27. Borzoi   28. Great Dane   29. Border Collie   30. Chihuahua   31. Old English Sheepdog

38. <u>THE HUMAN BODY</u>   1. Kneecap   2. Finger & toe bones   3. Lower jaw   4. Thigh bone   5. Collar bone   6. Breastbone   7. Shin bone   8. Shoulder bone   9. In the throat   10. In the pancreas   11. Above the kidneys   12. In the brain (at the base)   13. In the liver   14. In the mouth (salivary gland)   15. Heart   16. Eye   17. Brain   18. Lungs   19. Stomach   20. Nose   21. Ear   22. Kidney   23. Shoulder   24. Lower leg   25. Bottom   26. Chest   27. Upper arm   28. Head (or cheek)   29. Thigh   30 Back (upper)

39. <u>COUPLES</u>   1. On the Titanic   2. A singer with a band   3. Designed her wedding dress   4. Jazz   5. On a prayer   6. The Good Life   7. Had her beheaded   8. On ' I'm a celebrity get me out of here'   9. Waterloo station   10. Jennifer died of leukaemia   11. West Side Story   12. Georgie Fame   13. Pain in childbirth   14. Holland   15. Whoopi Goldberg   16. He had a stroke   17. Ice dancers on 'Dancing on Ice'   18. Tell Laura I love her   19. Mamma Mia   20. Torquay

40. <u>WORDS BEGINNING WITH Q</u>   1. Quail   2. Quasar   3. Quagmire   4. Quagga   5. Queen of my Heart   6. Queensferry   7. Quadrill   8. Quotient   9. Quartz   10. Quadrophenia   11. Quire   12. The Quiet Man   13. Qatar   14. To be in queer street   15. Quito   16. The Quantocks   17. Quest   18. Quatermass   19. Quentin   20. Quatro (Suzi)   21. Quaver   22. Quakers   23. Quaid (Dennis)   24. Quink   25. Q-ships or Q-boats   26. QVC   27. Quincy

41. <u>WORDS BEGINNING WITH U</u>   1. Uluru   2. Utopia (Road to.....)   3. Usurp   4. Ullswater   5. Ursine   6. The Untouchables   7. Ugley   8. Ulster   9. Umbria   10. Unchained Melody   11. Unicorn   12. (Liv) Ullmann   13. Ulveston   14. Uzbekastan   15. United Arab Emirites   16. Unforgiven   17. Una (Stubbs)   18. Up Pompeii   19. Ullapool   20. Under milk wood   21. Umbrella   22. Underneath the Arches   23. Una Paloma Blanca   24. Uhu glue   25. Umbra   26. Ulm

42. <u>ANSWERS FINISHING IN IC</u>   1. Chic   2. Colic   3. Ferric   4. Stoic   5. Tic   6. Emetic   7. Static   8. Nordic   9. Cubic   10. Aspic   11. Gaelic   12. Cosmic   13. Comic   14. Erotic   15. Gothic   16. Civic   17. Cyclic   18. Rustic   19. Septic   20. Doric OR Ionic   21. Relic   22. Music   23. Gallic   24. Vic   25. Acetic

43. <u>WORD ORIGINS</u>   1. Cornish   2. Arabic   3. Bengali   4. Welsh   5. Dutch   6. Jananese   7. French   8. Spanish   9. Finnish   10. Gaelic   11. Danish   12. French   13. Norwegian   14. Spanish   15. Zulu   16. Latin   17. Latin   18. Japanese   19. Cantonese   20. Welsh   21. Swedish   22. Hindi   23. Hebrew   24. Spanish   25. Bengali

44. <u>FAMOUS BOOKS WITHOUT VOWELS</u>   1. Lorna Doone   2. Vanity Fair   3. A Tale of Two Cities   4. The Da Vinci Code   5. Animal Farm   6. Ivanhoe   7. Wuthering Heights   8. The Satanic Verses   9. Brighton Rock   10. Alice in Wonderland   11. The Call of the Wild   12. Emma   13. The Day of the Triffids   14. Born Free   15. Lord Jim   16. Black Beauty   17. Barchester Towers   18. Moby Dick   19. Watership Down   20. Lucky Jim   21. Uncle Tom's Cabin   22. Treasure Island   23. To Kill a Mocking Bird   24. Lady Chatterley's Lover   25. The Thirty Nine Steps   26. Fifty Shades of Grey

45. <u>FLAG DESIGNS</u>   1. Saudi Arabia   2. New Zealand   3. South Korea   4. Canada   5. Malta   6. Brazil   7. Kenya   8. Liberia   9. Greece   10. South Africa   11. Cyprus   12. Jamaica   13. India   14. Afghanistan   15. Nepal   16. Vatican City   17. Lebanon   18. Sri Lanka   19. Pakistan   20. Portugal   21. Algeria   22. Australia

46. <u>LONDON UNDERGROUND</u>   <u>Colour</u> 1. Piccadilly   2. Victoria   3. Waterloo & City   4. Central   5. Metropolitan   6. Hammersmith & City   7. East London   8. Circle   9. Bakerloo   10. District   11. Docklands Light Railway   12. Jubilee   13. Northern   <u>Terminus</u> – 1. Piccadilly   2. Metropolitan   3. Jubilee   4. Northern   5. Central   6. District   7. Docklands Light Railway   8. East London   9. Victoria   10. Northern   11.District   12. District   <u>Stations</u> – 1. Victoria, Circle, District   2. Waterloo & City, Bakerloo, Northern, Jubilee   3. Northern, Victoria   4. Hammersmith & City, Circle, Metropolitan, Central.   <u>Extra questions</u>   1. Metropolitan   2. Victoria   3. The Fleet Line   4. He designed the Underground Map.

47. <u>BRITAIN'S COASTLINE</u>   1. Romney Marsh 2. Beachy Head   3. Selsey Bill   4. The Needles
5. Brownsea Island   6. Lulworth Cove   7. Lizard Point   8. St Michael's Mount   9. Lands End
10. Lundy Island   11. Gower Peninsular   12. Cardigan Bay   13. Anglesey   14. The Wirral
15. Isle of Walney   16. Isle of Man   17. Mull of Kintyre   18. Arran   19. Lewis   20. Shetlands
21. Holy Island   22. Farne Islands   23. Flamborough Head   24. Humber Estuary   25. The Wash
26. The Naze   27. Canvey Island

48. <u>PLACES IN BRITAIN 1</u>   1. Fort William   2. Skye   3. York   4. Southend   5. Middlesborough
6. Conwy   7. Colchester   8. Anglesey   9. Liverpool   10. Ulverston   11. Edinburgh   12. Lowestoft
13. Nottingham   14. Staffa   15. Lockerbie   16. Oxford   17. Gateshead   18. Norwich   19. Ayr
20. Cardiff   21. Plymouth   22. Aberdeen   23. Isle of Wight   24. Bath   25. Worcester
26. Hereford   27. Grantham   28. Chester

49. <u>PLACES IN BRITAIN 2</u>   1. Wilton   2. Canterbury   3. Winchester   4. The Shetlands
5. Huntingdon   6. Bristol   7. Inverness   8. Lindisfarne   9. Harlow   10. Brownsea   11. Dundee
12. Boscastle   13. Kendal   14. Gloucester   15. Isle of Man   16. Whitby   17. Gosport
18. Sheffield   19. Belfast   20. Bangor   21. Blackpool   22. Stoke on Trent   23. Wallsend
24. York   25. Grasmere   26. Llandudno   27. Salisbury   28. Penzance

50. <u>PLACES IN BRITAIN 3</u>   1. Lundy   2. Surrey   3. Glen Coe   4. Tay   5. Dorchester   6. Edinburgh
7. Chelmsford   8. Antrim   9. St Davids   10.Scotland   11. Liverpool   12. Wick   13. Bath   14. New
Forest   15. Rochdale   16. Peckham   17. Northern Ireland   18. Winchester   19. Padstow
20. Cockermouth   21. Leicestershire   22. Dartford   23. Rolls Royce   24. Dylan Thomas
25. Shropshire   26. Margate   27. Leeds   28. Dartmoor

51. <u>FOUR LETTER PLACES IN BRITAIN</u>   1. Aire 2. Avon   3. Bath   4. Bude   5. Bury   6. Deal
7. Diss   8. Down   9. Eton   10. Fife   11. Hove   12. Hull   13. Leek   14. Looe   15. Lydd   16. Mold
17. Nene   18. Ness 19. Oban   20. Peel   21. Rhyl   22. Ryde   23. Sale   24. Soho   25. Spey
26. Tees   27. Tyne   28. Ware   29. Wick   30. York

52 <u>PLACES IN ENGLAND</u>   1. Aintree Racecourse 2. Norfolk Broads 3. Lands End   4. Whitby
Abbey 5. Whipsnade Zoo 6. Humber Bridge 7. Osborne House 8. Tower of London 9. Old
Trafford Cricket Ground   10.Canterbury Cathedral   11. Lake District   12. Morcambe Bay
13. HMS Victory   14. Stonehenge   15. Royal Liver Building   16. Sherwood Forest   17. Dartmoor
18. National Motor Museum   19. New Forest   20. Windsor Castle   21. Brighton Pavilion
22. Wigan Pier   23. Wembley Stadium   24. Eden Project   25. Radcliffe Camera   26. Manchester
Airport   27. Silverstone   28. Blenheim Palace   29.Coventry Cathedral   30. Hadrian's Wall

53. <u>WORD PATTERN</u>   All the words have a double letter in them and are in alphabetical order. No
word has a double Q or Y.   1. Bazaar   2. Scrabble   3. Broccoli   4. Fiddler   5. Kleenex   6. Jiffy
7. Fraggle   8. Fishhook (This is a compound word and can be written as a single word)
9. Pompeii   10. Hajj   11. Trekker   12. Killers   13. Hammerhead   14. Fennel   15. Boom
16. Hippopotamus   17. IMPOSSIBLE   18. Warren   19. Hiss   20. Otter   21. Vacuum   22. Navvy
23. Powwow   24. Exxon   25. IMPOSSIBLE   26. Dizzy

54. <u>THE NUMBERS GAME</u>   1. 12   2. 78   3. 876   4. 23   5. 6   6. 600   7. 76   8. 24   9. 62
10. 63   11. 12   12. 1634   13. 5   14. 15   15. 3   16. 9   17. 10.5   18.88   19. 111   20. 8
21. 26   22. 26   23. 3   24. 64   25. 5   26. 12   27. 13   28. 105   29. 50   30. 12   31. 70

55. <u>MAP OF SOUTH AMERICA</u>   1. Belize 2. Guatemala 3. El Salvador 4. Honduras
5. Nicaragua 6. Costa Rica 7. Panama 8. Columbia 9. Venezuela 10. Guyana 11. Suriname
12. French Guiana 13. Ecuador 14. Peru 15. Brazil 16. Bolivia 17. Chile 18. Paraguay
19. Uruguay 20. Argentina

56. <u>MAP OF AFRICA</u>   1. Morocco 2. Algeria 3. Tunisia 4. Libya 5. Gambia 6. Sierra Leone
7. Liberia 8. Ivory Coast 9. Ghana 10. Nigeria 11. Cameroon 12. Central African Republic
13. Ethiopia 14. Somalia 15. Uganda 16. Kenya 17. Tanzania 18. Angola 19. Zambia
20. Mozambique 21.Namibia 22. Botswana 23. Zimbabwe 24. Madagaster 25. South Africa

57. <u>MAP OF THE GREAT LAKES</u>   L1. Lake Superior   L2. Lake Michigan   L3. Lake Huron   L4. Lake
Erle L5. Lake Ontario   A. Chigago   B. Detroit   C. Cleveland   D. Buffalo   E. Toronto
1. Minnesota 2. Iowa 3. Michigan 4. Ohio 5. New York

58. <u>INVENTERS</u>   1. Computer (early type called The Analytical Engine)   2. Light bulb   3. Cats Eyes   4. Dynamite   5. Photographic Film (NOT just photographs)   6. X-Rays   7. <u>Bagless</u> vacuum cleaner   8. Miner's safety lamp   9. Printing Press   10. Christmas Cards   11. Atom Bomb   12. Saxophone   13. Helicopter   14. Aqua-lung   15. Telephone   16. The Internet (World Wide Web)   17. Postage Stamp 18. Hovercraft   19. Wind-up Radio   20. Gramophone   21. Machine Gun   22. Radio Communication   23. Ball-point pen   24. Thermos or Vacuum Flask   25. Cinematography (Motion Pictures)   26. Television   27. Revolver   28. Phonograph and/or light bulb (in America)   29. Apple-Mac i-pod, i-phone, i-pad etc.   30. Hot-air Balloon   31. Crossword Puzzle   32. Steam Engine

59. <u>'BEFORE THEIR TIME'</u>   1. Killed by an arrow while hunting   2. Murdered   3. Beheaded   4. Executed by burning   5. Prime Minister assassinated by shooting   6. Typhoid   7. Motor-cycle accident   8. Aircraft 'lost' over the English Channel   9. Suicide by cyanide   10. Drug overdose   11. Air crash   12. Car crash   13. Suicide   14. Air crash   15. Drowned in a boating accident   16. Shot by his father   17. Fell down stairs, brain haemorrhage   18. Riding accident   19. AIDS   20. Motor-racing accident   21. Cancer   22. Skiing accident   23. Murdered by shooting   24. Brain haemorrhage after a fall   25. Hit by a speedboat   26. Collapsed and died after a skiing accident   27. Alcohol poisoning

60. <u>BRITISH PRIME MINISTERS & MPs</u>   <u>Prime Ministers</u> 1. Walthamstow West   2. Woodford   3. Warwick & Leamington   4. Bromley   5. Kinross & W. Perthshire   6. Huyton   7. Bexley   8. Cardiff SE   9. Finchley   10. Huntingdon   11. Sedgefield   12. Kirkcaldy & Cowdenbeath   13. Witney   <u>Other MPs</u> 1. Yeovil   2. West Bromwich   3. Sheffield Hallam   4. Falmouth & Camborne   5. Leeds East   6. Henley   7. Ross, Skye & Lochaber   8. Doncaster North   9. Rochdale   10. Chesterfield   11. Maidstone & The Weald   12. Crosby

61. <u>FIXED DATES ON THE CALENDAR</u>   1. 1stApril   2. 1stNovember   3. 2nd / 3rdNovember   4. 11thNovember   5. 22nd/ 23rdSeptember   6. 15thSeptember   7. 25thJanuary   8. 2ndJune   9. 6thJanuary 10. 5thNovember   11. 31stOctober   12. 31stDecember   13. 1stMay   14. 24thJune   15. 30thNovember   16. 1stMarch   17. 23rdApril   18. 17thMarch   19. 26thDecember   20. 15thJuly   21. 14thFebruary   22. 21st/ 22ndJune   23. 21stApril   24. 20th/ 21stMarch   25. 20th/ 21stDecember   <u>Other Days</u> 1. 4thJuly   2. 11thSeptember   3. 22ndNovember   4. 31stAugust   5. 8thDecember   6. 7thJuly   7a. Thursday   7b. Tuesday   8. Shrove Tuesday   9. Whitsun OR Whit Sunday

62. <u>CARS USED IN FILMS & TV (MATCH)</u>   1. Goldfinger   2. Ashes to Ashes   3. Fawlty Towers   4. Mr Bean   5. Ghostbusters   6. Dukes of Hazzard   7. Back to the Future films   8. Miami Vice   9. Harry Potter & the Chamber of Secrets   10. The Professionals   11. Life on Mars   12. The Sweeny   13. Starsky & Hutch   14. Laurel & Hardy films   15. Z-Cars   16. Austin Powers films   17. Morse   18. The Spy who Loved Me   19. The Italian Job   20. Open All Hours   21. Columbo   22. Knight Rider   23. The New Avengers   24. The Darling Buds of May   25. Keeping Up Appearances   26. Bergerac   27. Herbie Rides Again   28. The Saint

63. <u>FAMOUS ADDRESSES</u>   1. Stan & Hilda Ogden   2. The Simpsons   3. Dr. Crippen   4. Paddington Bear   5. John Lennon   6. The Boswells (Bread)   7. Fred & Rose West   8. Harry Potter & the Dursleys   9. Chancellor of the exchequer   10. Wallace & Gromit   11. Sponge Bob Square Pants   12. Brontë Family   13. Dr. Doolittle   14. Charles Dickens   15. Sherlock Holmes   16. Phil Mitchell   17. Steptoe & Son   18. Duke of Wellington   19. Miss Marple   20. Ewing Family (Dallas)   21. Tony Hancock   22. William Wordsworth   23. Batman   24. Sharon Tate & Roman Polanski   25. Victor Meldrew (One Foot in the Grave)   26. Noddy   27. Del & Rodney Trotter (Only Fools & Horses)   28. Reginald Christie (Murderer)   29. The American President (White House)   30. Superman (Clark Kent)   31. Donald Duck

64. <u>CRIME & CRIMINALS</u>   1. August   2. The Wests   3. Ipswich   4. Lord Lucan   5. Fanny Adams   6. Art Forgery   7. Drowned his victims in a bath   8. Brinks mat   9. Lorry driver   10. Dissolved his victims in acid   11. Jonathan Aitkin   12. Louie Mountbatten   13. Fingerprints   14. Barbara Windsor   15. Dr Crippen   16. Ruth Ellis   17. The Crown Jewels   18. Reginald Christie   19. Charles   20. Ross   21. Edward II   22. Mary Bell   23. Whitechapel   24. Stone of Scone   25. An IRA bomb   26. Millie Dowler

65. <u>**MOTORWAYS & A ROADS**</u>   1. London, Leeds   2. (Already given)   3. London, Southampton   4. London, Swansea   5. Birmingham, Exeter   6. Carlisle   7. Glasgow, Edinburgh   8. Edinburgh   9. London, Cambridge   10. Folkestone   11. Crawley   12. Portsmouth   13. London, Birmingham (Solihull)   14. Chester   15. Preston, Blackpool   16. Liverpool, Kingston Upon Hull   17. Preston   18. Edinburgh   19. Portsmouth   20. Holyhead   21. Kings Lynn   22. Great Yarmouth   23. Southend   24. Felixstowe

66. <u>**COMPANIES COUNTRY OF ORIGIN**</u>   1. Japan   2. Denmark   3. South Korea   4. Ireland   5. UK   6. France   7. USA   8. Germany   9. USA   10. USA   11. Hong Kong   12. South Korea   13. Sweden   14. USA   15. Japan   16. USA   17. France   18. Germany   19. Denmark   20. Switzerland   21. Finland   22. Italy   23. UK   24. USA   25. Holland   26. Germany   27.Switzerland   28. Spain   29. Holland & UK (either answer)   30. Czechoslovakia   31. Germany   32. Belgium

67. <u>**CLUES TO SWEETS & CHOCOLATE BARS**</u>   1. Lion Bar   2. Bournville Chocolate   3. Curly Wurly   4. Polo   5. Double Decker   6. Celebrations   7. Whole Nut   8. Whispa   9. Snickers   10. Roses   11. Liquorish   12. Love Hearts   13. Penguins   14. Dolly Mixtures   15. Club   16. Toffee Crisp   17. All Gold   18. Kit Kat   19. Mars   20. Bounty   21. Maltesers   22. Sherbet Fountain   23. Milk Tray   24. Quality Street   25. Flake   26. Fry's Turkish Delight   27. Murray Mints   28. Star Bar   29. Smarties   30. Fudge   31. Milky Bar   32. Flying Saucers

68. <u>**CLUES TO ANIMALS**</u>   1. Chameleon   2. Alligator   3. Pussycat   4. Lamb   5. Reindeer   6. Rat   7. Doggie   8. Ape   9. Bat   10. Cow   11. Lion   12. Teddy Bear   13. Frog   14. Horse(s)   15. Hippopotamus   16. Rabbit   17. Crocodile   18. Weasel   19. Walrus   20. (Black) Sheep   21. Mice(Mouse)   22. Elephant   23. Kitten(s)   24. Gibbon   25. Goat   26. Wolf   27. Kangaroo   28. Pig(s)   29. Bull   30. Puppy

69. <u>**CLUES TO BIRDS**</u>   1. Crane   2. Canary   3. Nightingale   4. Ostrich   5. Jackdaw   6. Goose   7. Mallard   8. Raven   9. Crow   10. Stork   11. Secretary Bird   12. Roadrunner   13. Budgerigar   14. Emu   15. Eagle   16. Sparrow   17. Swan   18. Kingfisher   19. Finch   20. Bluebird   21.Rook   22. Flamingo   23. Owl   24. Blackbird   25. Magpie   26. Pelican   27. Seagull   28. Penguin   29. Kookaburra   30. Falcon   31. Dodo

70. <u>**CLUES TO COLOURS**</u>   1. Yellow   2. Red   3. White   4. Brown   5. Green   6. White   7. Pink   8. Yellow   9. Purple   10. Blue   11. Red   12. Brown   13. Green   14. Black   15. White   16. Yellow   17. Black   18. Brown or Blue   19. Pink   20. Blue   21. Green   22. Yellow   23. Brown   24. Blue   25. Purple   26. Red   27. Black   28. White   29. Brown   30. Pink (or Blue)   31. Blue   32. Red

71. <u>**CLUES TO FLOWERS**</u>   1. Lavender   2. Snowdrop   3. Tiger Lily   4. Poppies   5. Foxgloves   6. Honeysuckle   7. Water Lilies   8. Rose   9. Buttercup   10. Dahlia   11. Lilac   12. Sunflower   13. Lily   14. Wallflower   15. Violet   16. Iris   17. Cherry Blossom   18. Dandelion   19. Edelweiss   20. Astor   21. Daisy   22. Snapdragon or Antirrhinum   23. Forget-me-not   24. Daffodil   25. Orchid   26. Lotus   27. Crocus

72. <u>**CLUES TO METALS**</u>   1. Brass   2. Lead   3. Solder   4. Titanium   5. Gold   6. Aluminium   7. Tin   8. Sodium   9. Nickel   10. Steel   11. Platinum   12. Zinc   13. Chrome or Chromium   14. Copper   15. Magnesium   16. Pewter   17. Amalgam   18. Plutonium   19. Calcium   20. Silver   21. Tungsten   22. Bronze   23. Potassium   24. Uranium   25. Mercury   26. Gun Metal   27. Arsenic

73. <u>**CLUES TO DAYS & MONTHS**</u>   1. April   2. Saturday   3. September   4. Saturday   5. Thursday   6. Monday   7. Tuesday   8. August   9. June   10. Sunday   11. Saturday   12. Saturday or Sunday   13. Monday   14. May   15. Friday   16. Sunday   17. Wednesday   18. May   19. June   20. Sunday   21. December   22. May   23. Sunday   24. Saturday   25. June   26. January or February   27. March   28. Tuesday   29. April   30. Thursday   31. May or December

74. <u>**CLUES TO WORLD TOWNS & CITIES**</u>   1. Tokyo   2. Chicago   3. Barcelona   4. Kuala Lumpur   5. Vienna   6. Dubai   7. Singapore   8. London   9.Amritsar   10. Rio De Janeiro   11. Giza   12. The Hague   13. Paris   14. St Petersburg   15. Milan   16. Venice   17. Dublin   18. Rangoon   19. Johannesburg   20. Hong Kong   21. New York   22. Rome   23. Beijing   24. Berlin   25. Washington   26. Geneva   27. Prague   28. Toronto   29. Athens   30. Brussels   31. Istanbul   32. San Francisco

75. **CLUES TO FRUIT VEGETABLES & HERBS** 1. Orange 2. Grapes 3. Kiwi 4. Strawberry 5. Banana 6. Lemon 7. Spinach 8. Gooseberry 9. Bean 10. Broccoli 11. Basil 12. Cherry 13. Coconut 14. Pineapple 15. Blackberry 16. Peach 17. Cabbage 18. Pawpaw 19. Parsley 20. Raspberry 21. Sage 22. Onion 23. Plum 24. Rocket 25. Blueberry 26. Marrow 27. Chicory 28. Potato 29. Rosemary 30. Lime 31. Melon

76. **CLUES TO PLACES IN LONDON** 1. Baker Street 2. Wimbledon Common 3. Old Kent Road 4. Shoreditch 5. Piccadilly 6. Victoria Station 7. The Mall 8. Birdcage Walk 9. Swiss Cottage 10. Earl's Court 11. Hackney 12. Shaftsbury Avenue 13. Hyde Park 14. Lambeth 15. The Strand 16. Richmond 17. Vauxhall 18. Nine Elms 19. Fleet Street 20. Whitechapel 21. Knightsbridge 22. Notting Hill 23. Marble Arch 24. Lewisham 25. King's Cross 26. Mile End 27. Poplar 28. Bond Street 29. Waterloo Station 30. Hatton Garden 31. Paddington Station 32. Soho

77. **CLUES TO COMPASS DIRECTIONS** 1. Oliver North 2. Way Out West 3. Westlife 4. Northern Lights 5. Clint Eastwood 6. South Park 7. Northampton 8. South Sudan 9. Rose West 10. South Georgia 11. Southend-on-Sea 12. Mae West 13. Westwood Ho! 14. Timothy West 15. Adam West 16. East 17 17. Sheena Easton 18. West Highland Terrier 19. West End Girls 20. East Grinstead 21. West Side Story 22. North by North-West 23. Beautiful South 24. Southsea 25. East of Eden 26. Due South 27. East Timor 28. Southfork 29. South Pacific 30. Joe South 31. West Virginia

78. **CLUES TO AMERICAN STATES** 1. New Hampshire 2. Wisconsin 3. Louisana 4. Hawaii 5. Indiana 6. California 7. Tennesee 8. New Jersey 9. Mississippi 10. Rhode Island 11. Georgia 12. Utah 13. Kentucky 14. Arkansas 15. Massachusetts 16. Alaska 17. Montana 18. Virginia 19. Maryland 20. Idaho 21. Iowa 22. Kansas 23. Texas 24. Colorado 25. North Carolina 26. Washington 27. Nebraska 28. Pennsylvania 29. Minnesota 30. Oklahoma 31. New Mexico 32. New York

79. **CLUES TO THINGS IN A SCHOOL** 1. Books 2. Football 3. Calculator 4. Pupils 5. Laboratories 6. (The) Piano 7. Protractor 8. The Stage 9. Pencil 10. Bell 11. Paper (Moon) 12. Crayons OR Coloured pencils 13. Teachers 14. Desks 15. Headmaster 16. Photocopier 17. Homework 18. Chalk 19. Dictionary 20. Gymnasium 21. Scissors 22. Paper clips OR staples 23. Chairs 24. Compass 25. Dinnerladies 26. Cloakroom 27. Pen 28. Globe 29. Playground 30. Rubber 31. Ruler

80. **CLUES TO THINGS IN A HOSPITAL** 1. Nurse 2. Thermometer 3. Laboratory 4. Drugs 5. Blood 6. Defibrillator 7. Wards 8. ECG 9. Patients 10. Oxygen 11. Midwife 12. Bandages 13. Bed Pan 14. Bed 15. Surgeon 16. X-Rays 17. Needle 18. Porter 19. Matron 20. Plaster of Paris 21. Trolley 22. Receptionist 23. Tablets 24. Pillow 25. Doctor 26. Stethoscope 27. Curtain 28. Pharmacy 29. Syringe 30. Theatre 31. Sterilizer